This poem is SPONSORED by...

Poems in the face of corporate power

Celebrating the 10th anniversary of Corporate Watch

www.corporatewatch.org.uk

Compiled and edited by **Claire Fauset**
Designed with **Stig**

Published by **Corporate Watch** UK
16b Cherwell Street, Oxford, OX4 1BG
United Kingdom
Email: claire@corporatewatch.org
www.corporatewatch.org.uk

© Corporate Watch (UK) 2007

All rights reserved.
Copyrights remain with the artists.

A catalogue record for this book is available
from the British Library

ISBN: 978-0-9553431-1-7

Covers printed on Trucard (made from a minimum of 50% post-consumer waste, elemental chlorine free, Forest Stewardship Council accredited) by **Kennet Print Ltd**, Unit 6, Hopton Industrial Estate, Devizes, Wiltshire SN10 2EU Tel: 01380 720049 www.kennetprint.co.uk

Pages printed on Cyclus paper (made from 100% post-consumer recycled waste, Eco-Management and Audit Scheme (EMAS) and EU Eco-label accredited) by **Antony Rowe Ltd**, Bumpers Farm, Chippenham, Wiltshire SN14 6LH
Tel: 01249 659705 www.antonyrowe.co.uk

CDs pressed by **Key Production Ltd**, 8 Jeffreys Place, London NW1 9PP
Tel: 020 7284 8800 www.keyproduction.co.uk

Introduction

In 2005 I wrote a poem 'And now a word from our sponsors...' attacking BP's efforts to portray itself as a caring, cultured and socially responsible company by sponsoring an array of prestigious art institutions in London. At the same time I was writing a report for Corporate Watch 'What's Wrong With Corporate Social Responsibility?' about how companies entrench their power by professing to have social consciences.

I've performed that poem to more people than have read my report, including many who would not otherwise have come across Corporate Watch's work. Also, I believe that the core of what I think about corporate greenwash is as clearly and passionately put across in those 27 lines of verse as in the 32 pages of analysis in the report.

So, having produced so much in the way of rigorous research, we decided our tenth birthday was high time to throw something else into the arena of radical writing.

Even though we argue our politics with clear logic and solid morality, it's not enough. For one thing, it is generally only listened to by people with an active interest in politics. But more than that, it's about appealing to our rational mind. That's the best bit of us to be charged with taking serious decisions, but it has no personality.

To win our battles we have to speak in a way that resonates somewhere deeper than the intellect. Poetry uses not just the meaning of words but their sound and rhythm; it uses not just logic but humour; it thumps a fist on the table, points an accusatory finger then flicks the Vs.

From the jongleurs to Johnny Rotten, poets have always had a political role articulating discontent, showing up the folly of the powerful and agitating for change. They can express the common feeling with a short sharp slap that challenges the powerful and emboldens the repressed.

This collection brings together radical anti-corporate poetry from over 60 talented poets. When I started out on the project I had no idea how the collection would take shape or even whether there was enough anti-corporate poetry out there to create a collection. It was a gamble, but one that clearly paid off.

As so many of the poems were written to be performed rather than read, there's a CD too. Some pieces are so performance orientated that they didn't work as well transcribed, so they're only on the CD.

There are poets in this anthology that have 'mainstream' reputations and have published numerous collections of their own work; there are poets from the vibrant spoken word scene that is establishing itself on both sides of the Atlantic; there are poems here from activists who write to understand and explain the world they live in and what they are fighting for.

I wanted to create a book that you could read from cover to cover and in the process be taken through Corporate Watch's analysis of why corporations are destructive, how they have power, how they use it, and how we can resist their dominance. I'm proud to say that I think this book does that job very well, and with so many strong voices that it feels like a declaration from a strident and colourful movement. These poets aren't taking that semi-apologetic tone anti-capitalists often use. They know they're right and they're shouting it loud and proud with brazen razor wit and bare-faced cheek.

I also wanted a collection that would be used by campaigners to get their message across, with poems that could be performed at rallies, and songs to sing while locked onto the gates of a nuclear power station. Preaching to the choir is an underrated activity; we all need poetry to galvanise us in our dissent, to motivate and inspire us, and to make us think, as well as to entertain us. I hope people will take this book with them on actions!

Dipping into this book it reads like a lively gig; it has power and punch and irreverence. It gives a sense of living in our time of late capitalist madness. In 50 years time, when the world is changed utterly, people may read this book and understand how it is for us now, living in the nonsensedrome.

I don't believe that poetry alone can change the world. But we can, and this book gives us a hefty kick up the arse.

Claire Fauset
December 2006

Acknowledgements

I would like to thank all the poets who sent their work in for consideration, as well as those poets who are published here. Many thanks also to all those who have been involved with organising launch events for the book. Thanks to Will Holloway, Todd Swift, Alan Buckley and Merrick for their support and enthusiasm which gave me the confidence to go ahead with the project right at the beginning, and for their editorial help throughout. Thanks to Stig for designing the book. Thanks also to Neil at Kennet Print, Dan Raymond Barker at New Internationalist, Mahalia, and everyone who made this project possible.

Contents

iii   Introduction by *Claire Fauset*

v   Contents

ix   I Did Not Speak Out - *Will Holloway*

1   Part one - How it works

1   How it works - *Alan Buckley*
2   Free market forces - *Helên Thomas*
3   Even the Starship *Enterprise* is getting grounded - *Heidi Greco*
4   Repossession - *Mario Petrucci*

6   Part two - Posh gits in suits

6   Inspirational speeches No. 1 : The Chief Executive - *Dave Morgan*
8   The Worst - *Mario Petrucci*
9   A game of two halves - *Elvis McGonagall*
11   Portrait of the Boss shaking hands with himself - *Kevin Higgins*
12   Memo to all counterfeit citizenz - *Alistair Stewart*
13   Occupy the managing directors - *Christian Zorka*
14   Trade not Aid - *Alan McClure*
16   Imploring a chain store - *Paul Spencer*
18   Scream - *Matthew Herbert*
20   Rhyme for Debt Times - *Emma Phillips*
21   I'm gonna boycott Body Shop - *Rapunzel Wizard*
22   Capital accumulation - *Will Holloway*
23   It's not an exact science - *Michelle Green*
26   And now a word from our sponsors... - *Claire Fauset*
27   What would you do for money? - *Kate Evans*

31 Part three - Thinking outside the box

- 31 Presentation Two at the Management Skills Development Workshop of the Acme Packaging Company - *David Bateman*
- 34 Corporate College - *Ken Champion*
- 35 Financial Affairs - *Nick Toczek*
- 37 www.startuppoem.com - *Jim Thomas*
- 40 If (rebranded) - *Luke Wright*
- 41 For those in peril in the City - *Josh Ekroy*
- 42 I have decided - *Alistair Noon*
- 43 Exit strategy - *Josh Ekroy*

45 Part four - Advertising will eat the world

- 45 Flogging tat - *Steve Tasane*
- 46 Advertiser's dream - *Jeffrey Mackie*
- 47 excerpt from The Occupation - *Paul Maltby*
- 49 Advertising will eat the world - *Adrian Mitchell*
- 50 On not taking up the agency's offer - *Alistair Noon*
- 51 Selling out - *Christian Zorka*
- 52 Hype - *Heidi Greco*
- 53 Pioneers, O Pioneers! - *Adrian Mitchell*
- 54 Memo to Barbie: Re the breakup - *Janis Butler Holm*

55 Part five - Television will not be Revolutionised

- 55 Television will not be revolutionised - *Ben Mellor*
- 58 The Bible according to Rupert Murdoch - *Attila the Stockbroker*
- 59 Potato - *Rosemary Harris*
- 61 That movie was so to die for - *Gregg Mosson*

62 Part six - This land is not your land

- 62   On not being beholden to random investors - *Christian Zorka*
- 63   This land's not your land - *Elvis McGonagall*
- 65   Dreaming on empty - *Heather Taylor*
- 66   Investment - *Aoife Mannix*
- 67   My pen has a name - *Spencer Cooke*
- 68   The Oil and Gas University - *Todd Swift*
- 69   These Gifts (ii) - *B R Dionysius*
- 70   Corporate Olympics - *T Troughton*
- 71   Swimming hole - *Mark Gunnery*
- 72   River - *Janet Vickers*
- 73   Monopoly - *Cath Morris*
- 75   Property - *Aoife Mannix*
- 76   Steal this poem - *Claire Fauset*
- 78   An open letter to enclosure - *Spencer Cooke*

79 Part seven - Plastic man

- 79   Plastic man - *Mark Gwynne Jones*
- 81   Seven signs of ageing - *Philip Jeays*
- 83   Cannibals of the western world - *Nick Toczek*
- 84   Excerpt from KnockBack 'The magazine for women who aren't silly bitches on a diet' - *Marie Berry*
- 85   Dead Meat - *Ewuare X. Osayande*
- 87   Ethical consumer - *Sheena Salmon*
- 88   Don't buy it - *Danny Chivers*
- 91   Book shopping - *Christian Zorka*

93 Part eight - Have a Job ™

- 93   Have a Job™ - *Merrick*
- 95   New Mills - *Penny Broadhurst*
- 97   Then... - *Ebele Ajogbe*
- 98   Daddy had a three year head cold - *Michelle Green*
- 100   The Conference of the (underemployed) birds - *B R Dionysius*
- 102   The Commuter's Song: 7/7, 9/11 - *George Roberts*
- 105   £8000/year≥ - *Michelle Green*

107 Part nine - Living in the Nonsensedrome

107   Seven sleepers - *K Simpson*
109   The long drive - *Vincent Tinguely*
111   Shoplifters recruitment drive - *Rapunzel Wizard*
113   The Klepto Dance - *Steve Tasane*
115   Gotham begins - *Emma Lee*
116   Lost in live streaming - *Helen Moore*
118   Positive images of gherkins - *Josh Ekroy*
119   The constitution of stars - *M T C Cronin*

121 Part ten - Beyond the mall

121   Beyond the mall - *David Rovics*
123   Bring down the garden centres - *Rachel Pantechnicon*
124   Changing the World - *John Hoggett*
126   resist.pl - *Charlie Harvey*
128   *from* Characters out in their thousands - *Ceri Buck*
129   The day the world stopped turning - *Rob Gee*
131   After the revolution - *David Rovics*
133   Life's a beach - *Marc Jones*

135 The poets

146   What is Corporate Watch?

148   Other publications by Corporate Watch

I Did Not Speak Out

First they came for the Jews
but I did not speak out
because I am an Artist
and I don't want to turn what I do
into mere propaganda.

Then they built gigantic missiles,
enough of them to destroy the Earth,
but I did not speak out
because Art is interested
only in what is eternal.

Then they melted the icecaps
and swamped the cities
but I did not speak out
because Literature is about
the intricate paradoxes of the heart,

in other words: adultery amongst the intelligentsia.
History is rising in waves
so I can't understand why
Poetry is on the beach, shouting:
Back, waves, go back! I command you!

Will Holloway

Part one - How it works

How it works
(A 27-line treatise on the dynamics of international capitalism)

According to someone
on the radio
this is how they catch monkeys
in India.

Big glass jar, narrow top.
Put a banana in it.

Monkey sees banana.
Monkey puts hand in jar.
Monkey grabs banana.
Monkey can't remove hand

without letting go of banana,
and is so attached -

to the idea of having that banana -
that it doesn't run away,
but keeps struggling
to get the banana out,

even as the man emerges
with the big sack.

Silly monkey! You almost piss yourself
laughing, as you sit in your shiny car -
one of several hundred lined up two by two

in the stationary queue
outside the retail park.

You won't believe our offers on plasma screen TVs!
We're practically giving them away!
Hell, you barely hear the rustle of cloth

as it slips past your ears.

Alan Buckley

Free Market Forces

Buy that! Want this? What's that? Want it? Go on, you need it. You're worth it. Why not? This month's must have. You can't be seen without it. What, not got one? God! You're worthless. Nobody loves you. Nobody wants you. Get it? Got that? What if you dropped that? What if you break it? Better buy a warranty. Better get a spare. Be prepared. Buy some extra bits. Now you need an add on. Come on! Better get a move on. Oops, now it's obsolete. Better get an upgrade. Yours is old. You're out of mode. Better get the new mould. Remodelled, repriced, re-sold. What's that? Wrong colour? Got scratched. Take it back. Better get a better one. But hang on! That cost a few bob. What if you get robbed? Better buy insurance. Better fix a fence. Get a gate. Get alarmed. Get armed. Join the neighbourhood. Watch. Buy a better watch. Better than your neighbour: Mrs Jones. She's so chic. Collagen and cheek bones. Fixed loans. Sticks and stones. You're going to die alone. Better buy a mobile phone, an i-pod and a Rolex. I bet you don't get much sex. Work out where's your six pack? Join a gym or get pissed? Watch your weight. Lose don't gain. Mind the gap. Take the train. Watch yourself. Avoid a sprain. Break your wrist. Here's the twist. Get a lawyer. Be a victim. Get a counsellor. Get neurosis, necrotosis. Get a second diagnosis. Open wide. Got halitosis? Better buy this. Gives you fresh breath. Butter wouldn't melt. Yes! I beat the breath test. Buy big butts and bouncing breasts. Soft touch? That's the acid test. Bigger, better, faster. More! Get a gun. Buy a war. Build a wall. Build a barrier. Buy a harrier jet. Get a contract. Make a killing. Market forces. We're all willing. Free to pay. Never, never. What you say? What's the cost? Just one dollar. Every day. Bargain.

Helên Thomas

Even the Starship *Enterprise* is getting grounded

We won't be remembered for traffic lights or shopping malls
the number of gadgets in our kitchens. I think
they'll remember us for ruining a planet, for-
getting there'd be people here after we're gone.

Today's morning paper said the corner shop is closing.
A place where you could get supplies, still untarnished
food. A store where you could choose which clump
of raisins look the best. Ask for only eighty grams,

please. Tradition dies so easy in a world where profit rules,
where greed is the closest word to God.
Next week they'll be scraping off the final episode
the last nest of ducklings from beside the quiet pond,

hidden in the park across the road. Making a space
where the Wal-Mart's going to be. Caribou are falling
through holes in softened ice, and look out. It isn't even

summer.

Heidi Greco

Repossession

Down the long leg of the catwalker fishnet melts

to meshwork tobacco spittle. A black liquid garter.
Asphalt picks itself up — each scaly skin spread
between kerbstones is pulling free with a bass

pop. Every city suddenly a kicked nest of adders
coiling together into a spitting rope of pitch.
All along their spines household molecules un-

crack — hydrocarbon vertebrae whose Lego atoms
snap back into line in a chiropracty of electron-volts.
Cars at last cough up. Judder to a stop. Dig ignition-

deep to sputter swart apologies across the crisp white
shirts of their hosts. And every sump on its scrap-heap
bumps and boils its box-black kettle — rejoices openly

as through the stratosphere water-vapour and dioxide
recombine: weave fine mists of oil to drop charred
tapeworms of cirrus. Videos slime in the hand like

jumbo choc-ices. CDs in the rack pucker and shrink
to mushy black peas. Dentures gum up the works
jarred into toothless gaga. Those precise blocks

and avenues of electronics crinkle dark and
mediaeval. In the fast lane of the bowling alley
a caviar cannonball splashes ten full bottles of

devil's milk — while those of the mobile who gas
this world down to its last nook into Porlock hell
shriek as they peel hot tar from lobes — Yes every

biro mothball racquet sags bleeds gutters
till the black string vest of tributaries resolves —
untangles towards tonsured ozone.   Finally

we notice. On satellite-replays Presidents track
their sloe'd candyfloss economies writhing round
earth's spindle — are caught on camera in black lip-

stick salve leaning to kiss the screen goodbye — and for
that moment the globe has a single gathering purpose
as a girl glances up from her fractions to witness

those filaments merge to a mother of twisters —
merge and rise and take her place. She watches
the whole black mass lift up and out into daytime

where it balls itself — steadies a wobbling edge
against blue to sling there its low fat circle. Crude
and glossy. She sees the birth of the full black moon

that lights our ways with dark.

Mario Petrucci

Part two - Posh gits in suits

Inspirational speeches No. 1 : The Chief Executive

I'm your Chief Executive
No need to feel unease
I'm here to turn this place around
Not bring it to its knees

I value your opinion
Feel free to disagree
It's healthy to have dialogue
Stand up and challenge me

(Too many bad suits
Too much lunchtime drinking
Too many old farts
Too much old thinking)

My door is always open
Approach me without fear
People who are positive
Are always welcome here

We might cut out some dead wood
Of course we will be fair
I've always valued loyalty
(How old did you say you were?)

Let's have a flatter structure
We'll start right at the top
(Anyone upset you?
Know someone you'd like to shop?)

Or maybe on the factory floor
Things seem a little slow
Let's re-engineer our processes
(That shower will have to go)

Downsizing will be minimal
Volunteers will get a package
(Resisters will be atomised
And reduced to nervous wreckage)

I know you've all got mortgages
So your partner's at death's door
Our shareholders have problems too
It's not a charity we're working for

(Too many time servers
Too many mickey takers
Too many sick notes
Too many rule breakers)

You can talk to me of unions
But it's me who keeps you fed
Know which side your toast is buttered
(Or your toast will be brown bread).

What we need is marketing
And lots of media hype
I want people who look the part
(Long legs, power suits,
    you know the type)

I want you to remember
The customer is king
You're only here to meet his needs
(Your needs don't mean a thing)

You will be given targets
How you get them I don't care
I want to see your outputs rise
I want to know you're there

(Too many has-beens
Too many whingers
Too many liberals
Too many gingers)

I want people with ambition
You're not paid to play it fair
I want pit bulls not chihuahuas
It's dog eat dog out there

I'm always up for new ideas
Shared over corporate dinners
A couple of bottles of Cristal
Will make us feel like winners

(Keep 'em lean and hungry
Offer 'em the earth,
Buy 'em off with promises
See what they're really worth)

There'll be lots of opportunity
In this new look company
You could have a rosy future
If you see things as I see

Yes I'm your Chief Executive
No need to feel unease
I'm here to turn this place round
Not bring it to its knees

Dave Morgan

The Worst

He wants a four-wheel drive but not the traffic
Assumes he'll wear the trousers - and the jacket

Won't brook immigrants (takes their labour)
Swims with dolphins then bulk-buys tuna

Wants enraptured audience till he wants to be alone
Wants the caviar mistress and a shepherd-pie home

Expects to have the choice and always to be chosen
Will pyramid-sell eleven for the baker's dozen

Assumes that anything he's about to say
will always hold at the end of the day

Will ride each gravy train First Class
or else use his elbows to accommodate his arse

Buys shares in uranium and futures in lead
Says a bullet with his name on it

is a hole in your head

Mario Petrucci

A game of two halves

Let's make poverty history
Let's be a force for good
Let's re-distribute all the wealth
Let's be like Robin Hood
Let's have no more paupers
Let's eradicate the rich
Let's empty out the bank account
Of Roman Abramovich
Let's syphon off his profits
Let's overthrow the petrol tsar
Let's give all his roubles back
To the workers of the USSR
Let's ask Jose Mourinho
"What's the Portuguese for poor?"
Let's cut his Amex card in two
Let him manage Stenhousemuir
Let's shove Sky TV where The Sun don't shine
Let Rupert Murdoch's empire fall
Let's reclaim the people's game
Let's take back our ball
Let's drop Ashley Cole down a deep dark hole
'Til he agrees that greed is wrong
Then we'll pay him 60 grand a week
In Vietnamese dong
Let's kidnap Malcolm Glazer
Singing "Soccer's going gnome!"
Let's bastardise his merchandise
Let's sell The Bobby Charlton Comb
Let's raid Wayne Rooney's piggy bank
Let's put him in a fucking rage
Let's make him work with Gordon Fucking Ramsay
For the minimum fucking wage
Let's stop spending money on sweet FA
Let Sven Goran Eriksson disappear
Let's fold him up in a flatpack

This poem is SPONSORED by...

And stack him on a shelf in Ikea
Let's find a check-out job at Tesco's
For Rio Ferdinand
Let's stick his mercenary contract
Up his Rio Grande
Let's ransack Beckingham Palace
Let's give their bling to charity
Let's burn the mock-tudor mansions
Of football's aristocracy
Let's drive all their Ferraris
Over Beachy Head
Let's de-rail their gravy train
Let them take the bus instead
Let's ignore their tabloid sex romps
And champagne charlie songs
Let's dismiss their Double-D-list wives
In permatans and Prada thongs
Let the VIPs drink Bovril
Let their seats be cold and hard
Let's rip up their red carpet
Let's show them the red card
Let's wind up Football plc
Let's give the board P45's
Let's stop fat corporate bastards
Eating all the pies
Let's kick-off the revolution
Let have-nots have the final score
Let's hear "Manchester United nil
    Partick Thistle 4"
Let's invest Das Kapital
Let's end left-wing fatigue
Then poverty will be history
When there's a socialist premier league

Elvis McGonagall

Part two - Posh gits in suits

Portrait of the Boss shaking hands with himself

So busy shaking hands with yourself
you miss in children's laughter
the universe warning you; never get it
when sidekicks leave post-its saying:
"Gone to live in North Korea",
or suggest your strategy

for the next shareholders' meeting should be
to do a little interpretive dance
to "Fanny (Be Tender With My Love)"
by the Bee Gees; nor spot
all around you briefcases fondly

remembering poverty - Spanish whiskey
on collapsing afternoons - and dreaming,
as once more they wave you off on holiday,
of a white mini-bus going off the motorway,
an Hawaiian shirt finally quiet.

Kevin Higgins

Memo to all counterfeit citzenz

do not interfere with supervisors
billionaires
or share holders
unless of course
they need some lunch money
remember, they are headlined as
geniuses of risk
their sons & daughters heirs to kingdoms
please portray as philanthropists
professional, competitive
officers, delegators
sponsors

STRICTLY NO QUESTIONS WITHOUT NOTICE

Alistair Stewart

Occupy the managing directors

sometimes
the best thing
to do
is to paint
your nails black
while watching
daytime tv.

there are certainly
people who would
do less
damage
that way.

unfortunately
they're
awfully insecure
about their
masculinity
and are unlikely
to do such things.

Christian Zorka

Trade not Aid

I was walking on the seashore when I heard a fearful cry
I looked out across the water where a man was drifting by
"You've got to help," he shouted, "there's a lifebelt in your reach,
If you throw it to me quickly I'll get back onto the beach!"
I hastily began to do exactly what he said
When a little word of warning made its way into my head.

"You reckon this will help," I said, "that is what you believe,
But to trust short-term solutions here is hopelessly naive.
You think the belt will save you, and for now perhaps it would,
But to teach a faulty lesson here would do more harm than good.
You want something for nothing, and that just is not the way
In the sophisticated economic climate of today,
You need trade!
You need trade, not aid,
You need trade!
I can't help until you've paid,
You say that you're in trouble and my help is all you need,
But a culture of dependency is all that it would breed!"

"What's wrong with you, you maniac?" he answered with a yell,
"I'm drowning in the ocean and there's nothing here to sell!
We can talk about your theories when I'm back upon the shore,
Now just throw the bloody lifebelt out, I beg you, I implore!
You have it in your power and you know that if you can,
You've a moral obligation to assist your fellow man!"

I told him "You are selfish, this is difficult for me;
You think a drowning person is a pleasant thing to see?
You shouldn't be in the water if you haven't learned to swim!"
He said "You no good lousy bastard, it was YOU who pushed me in!"
This kind of moral blackmail made me look at him aghast,
And say "There really is no virtue now in dwelling on the past,
You need trade!
You need trade, not aid,
You need trade!
I can't help until you've paid,
You say that you're in trouble and my help is all you need
But a culture of dependency is all that it would breed!"

"Don't be so pessimistic," I advised him, "you are rich!
the sea in which you're drowning must be lowping full of fish!"
"If that's what you're relying on," he said, "to judge my wealth,
Then you know that I have nothing, for you caught them all yourself."
I said "Well, you can't argue with the laws of competition,
You were wasting time by drowning when you should have been out fishin'."

When finally he died, I said "My brother, I will miss you,
But maybe more importantly, you've highlighted an issue.
Drowning is a menace, and believe me, now you're gone,
I'll be on the phone to Geldof, Ultravox and Elton John.
We'll organise a concert so that everyone can see
That drowning is a problem, we should make it history,
Using trade!
Using trade, not aid,
Good free trade!
the greatest plan we've ever made.
You say that you're in trouble and you say that you're in need,
but a culture of dependency's a rotten thing to breed
Yes, you say that you're in trouble and my help is all you need,
But a culture of dependency is all that it would breed."

Alan McClure

Imploring a Chain Store

traditional Irish tune: "The Kesh Jig"

A chain store arrived it was shiny and plastic,
With products inside that were truly fantastic,
The music was pumping the customers streamed,
The lighting was dazzling the packaging gleamed,

I marched straight inside it with no hesitating,
And up to the manager's desk without waiting,
I placed all my money in piles before him,
And down on my knees I began to implore him.

The first thing I ask is for half of this cash,
To go straight to the boss with the biggest moustache,
To help him to keep up his standard of living,
A most noble use for the money I'm giving.

The next subdivision a sizeable chunk,
You can spend on promoting these piles of junk,
If you teach me to want what you've got here for sale,
Then I'll buy some more every day without fail,

The reason I've brought all this cash I'm investing,
Is just to help out with the things I'm requesting,
With ev'ry new product I bring to the till,
I've another small wish for your boss to fulfill.

I want you to spend it on bribes and donations,
From small borough councils to United Nations,
I want you to buy up some small local farms,
And invest in a firm selling missiles and arms.

Please attack your suppliers and drive down their prices,
And squeeze out the small guy with ruthless devices,
Build private armies to guard what you steal,
And cry if a poor person shoplifts a meal.

I'm asking your business to buy a machine,
That's designed to pollute things that used to be clean,
Then invest all the rest in some corporate group,
So you keep it locked up in your Stock Exchange loop.

Build up your company, stack up your shelves,
And then take all our money to keep for yourselves,
Well that's what we actually ask you to do,
As we cheerfully hand over money to you.

Paul Spencer

Scream

i
They promise *Environmental Action*
for the ice cream eating faction
Social consciousness at your leisure
Nice capitalism - no pain, just pleasure
50 Ways to Promote Peace at your fingertips
Hush - never mind the exploitation of their *PG Tips*
You can *Lick Global Warming* with your *Chubby Hubby*
A world of happy cows, moose and pines - nothing's grubby
Surely nothing this good
Can leave you worried about becoming *Phish Food*
Drown
your fears in *Chocolate Fudge Brownie*
We're all in it together
Whatever the weather
Just you, me, Ben, Jerry and your money
Open the tub, no saccharine taste, sweet as honey
Eat your way to salvation
Forget Unilever's market domination

ii
You can have over fifty flavours of ice cream
But if you don't have one, single, powerful dream
You may as well give up and go back to bed
And wait for the frozen sensation to spread
Behind Vermont hippies lies a huge corporation
With their doctrine of greed and moral sanitation -
Domestos kills all ethical objections dead
But don't you worry your pretty little head
Have a night in with a tub of *Chunky Monkey*
Pretend everything's fine, hip, cool and funky
Just don't think a thought, just don't rock the boat
Try a new flavour, watch TV, 'text us your vote'

Whatever you're looking for, however it's measured
You won't find it buried in *Berried Treasure*
No significant journey's powered by frozen *Fossil Fuel*
Life's a storm on an ocean not a day by the pool
What's it to be? What choice do you make?
Do you want to get real? Can you bear the heartache?
Listen to words from old *'Cherry' Garcia*
and you might find it's not just some *Half Baked* idea
He said "Somebody has to do something"
So breathe life to your hope and let it take wing
Where do you want to find your Nirvana?
In the struggle for justice or in *Chocolate Carb Karma*
If you take what the corporations give you and feel grateful yet dead
You may as well give up and go back to bed

So, *Peanut Buttercups,* whatever you dream
Remember, justice wants you for a sunbeam
If we take back our power there's a glimmer of hope
We don't need no celebrity, no icons, no pope,
We don't need no president nor anyone that's prime
Let's take back our power and make this our time
We don't need them telling us what's right from wrong
That's like someone else singing our song
When our own voice is so beautiful
When our own voice is so very powerful

The Earth will thank you
The Earth will send you love letters

Matthew Herbert

Rhyme for Debt Times

(To the tune of Oranges and Lemons)

We'll make you happy, sings the banker at Abbey
Our debt is best, cries the bank of Nat West
Borrow from me, exclaims HSBC
We'll restore your pride, if you join Nationwide
A great mortgage planner if you sign with Britannia
The third world can fester, hums Alliance and Leicester
Life is not hard when you use Barclaycard
We'll all give you credit, though you survive in debit
The future is red, cut a deal with Egg
Interest free spending for an unhealthy ending
Lend us your sons, for our child trust funds
Here comes a loan to rip off the poor
Here comes a bailiff to show you the door.

Emma Phillips

I'm gonna boycott Body Shop

Anita Roddick the greedy cow
Has sold out to L'Oreal
That animal testing bunch of cocks
So I'm gonna boycott Body Shop.

L'Oreal's part owned by Nestlé
Who kill four thousand babes a day
With their powdered milk, to make it stop
I'm gonna boycott Body Shop.

So in part to stop the corporate scum
But mainly as I'm a soap dodging bum
Who never bought their fragrant rot
I'm gonna boycott Body Shop.

Rapunzel Wizard

Capital accumulation

I dreamt that I met a man in an expensive suit
pushing a wheelbarrow made of human bones.

Its handles were two long femurs,
its sides were made of ribs
and all the bones were as yellow as a pub ceiling.

I asked:
"Where are you going with your wheelbarrow?"
He replied:
"To my palace on the hill."

I looked up and I could see his palace.
It was also made of bones,
millions of them, phalanges, metacarpals, skulls,
all human, all yellow.

I asked:
"Who are you that you have accumulated so many bones?"
He replied:
"I am Mr. Benson-and-Hedges."

I asked:
"Then why is your wheelbarrow empty?"
He replied:
"Because tonight I have come for your bones."

And even as I awoke
my hand was patting the carpet for the lighter.

Will Holloway

It's not an exact science

It's a put your hands over your ears
    erase your fears science

It's a leech under the skin
    suck the blood demons within science

It's a thin science

a hide the blister packs in the bin science

It's a one way chemical pathway
through   your   brain   to sane   science

a fill in the form again science

A sit in the waiting room
    for free samples
don't think about the test groups
negative examples
general practitioners on three hours sleep science

It's a holistic help don't come cheap science
A drop your jaw and make the leap
                      flavour of the week science

It's a tick box analysis
    black hole paralysis
paroxetine to quiet your scream science

it's a monotone dream science.

A habit forming trip to the grey zone
The space between the channels

The buzz at the edge of earshot
   pain clot science

It's a passive robot
   tab under the tongue
to lower the pound of your heart
push you together
      then tear you -
    hold onto your soul
    with both hands
    hold on with both hands science

It's a desert tongue hung
high in the back of your throat
Ambition dried
    to the hem of your coat
Salt stains on your new shoes
everything to lose science

not a cheap cigarettes and booze science

A clean lined laboratory approved
   profit perforated
     margins   infused   with
on-site employee health spas
stock incentives
and a real artificial lake
    for
  when
    you
       take
    your break
       science

a taste so fake science

It's fifteen years old
    sat in a hot bath
    opening up a wrist
    pumping fist
That's not our problem
they were always at risk science

    (put your hands over your ears erase your fears)

It's twice the urge to slice

    (hands over your ears hands over your ears)

in test groups of healthy people

    (overyrearsoveryrearsover)

under the age of eighteen

And that's a fact

It is not
an exact
science

Michelle Green

And now a word from our sponsors...

This poem was written for the Art Not Oil exhibition, an art gallery opposing BP's sponsorship of a number of cultural institutions in London.

This poem is sponsored by BP.
The company is delighted to be collaborating on this project,
continuing its commitment to education and the arts,
as part of its Sustainability programme.

This poem is sponsored by BP.
Trees will be planted to offset the greenhouse gas emissions
that the poet farted whilst composing this piece.

This poem is sponsored by BP
There will be no mention of spills, rigs or drills.
The words 'Colombia' and 'death squads' will not appear in the same sentence.
'Petroleum' will feature only when accompanied by the word 'Beyond'.

This poem is sponsored by BP.
Please take one of our brochures.
We have many exciting initiatives in our pipelines.
Please read our 'Tips on Greener Motoring'.
Remember, big companies are doing what they can,
but it's down to the consumer to drive the market towards sustainability.

This poem is sponsored by BP.
It will present a clean, friendly image.
There will be no dark corners.
A wash of green will be liberally applied.

This poem is sponsored by BP.
Don't you get it?
There's nothing to see.
Move along.
Everything's just fine.

Claire Fauset

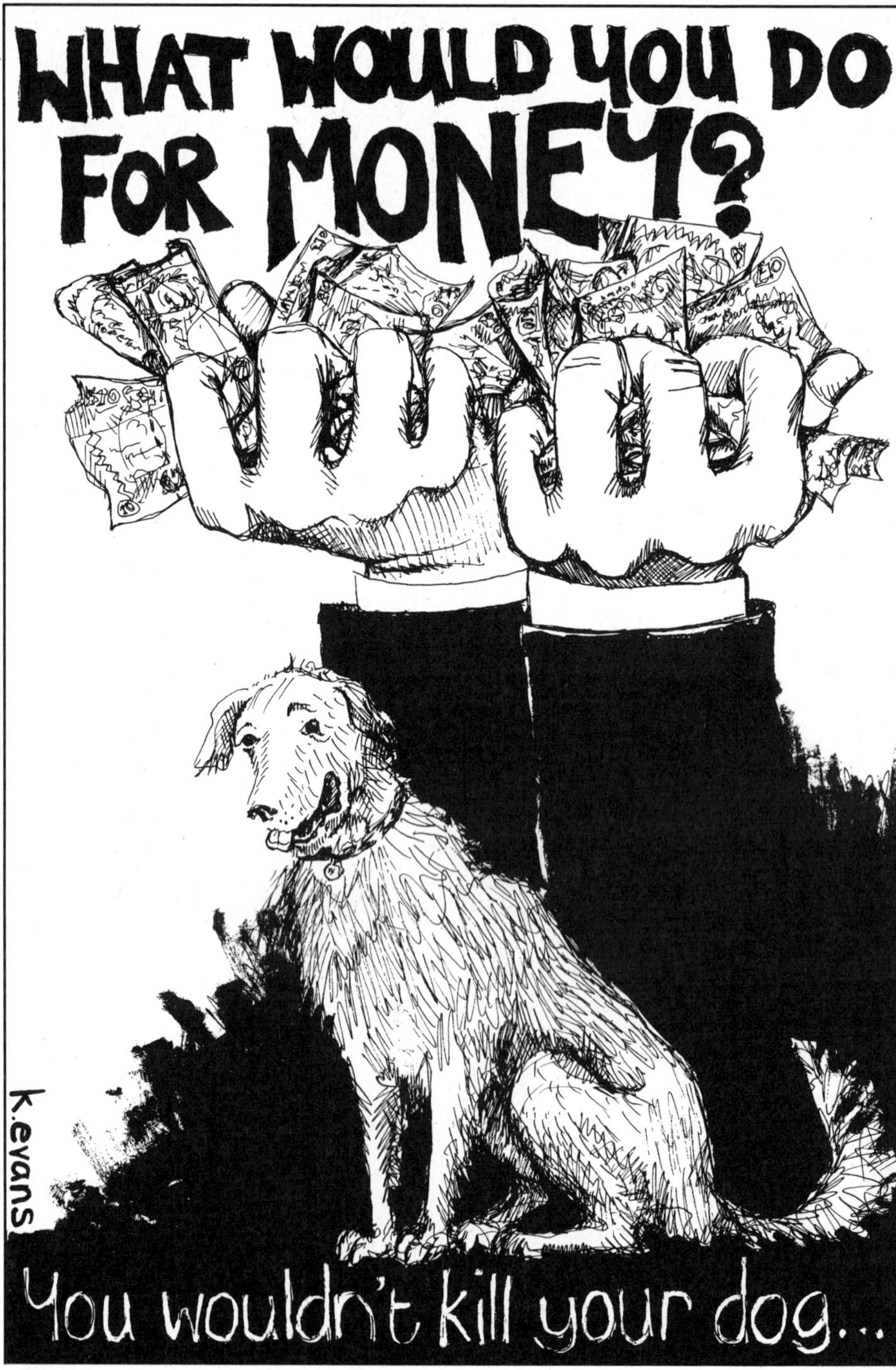

This poem is SPON$ORED by...

but the wolf in the forest, running free
finds the woodland depleted
the last tree cut for timber...

the gazelle on the grasslands
can see the vast spread
of man on the land

listen
seabirds
and songbirds cannot be heard
Now look at your hands
Tell me what do you see?

WHAT WOULD YOU DO FOR MONEY?
you wouldn't kill your lover...

Part two - Fat gits in suits

28

would you kill another's?

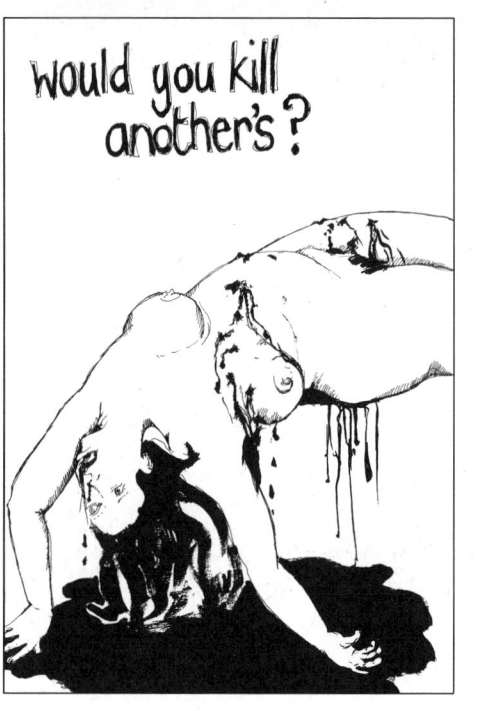

money buys the guns that keeps the arms trade going

when the bloody cycle's done the same money's in your pocket

disease and malnutrition courtesy of Third World debt.

How blinkered is your vision?

There's the bank there on the High Street

Go and buy a ticket for the lottery

pleased that a penny goes to charity.

WHAT WOULD YOU DO FOR MONEY?

You wouldn't kill your children...

29

This poem is SPON$OR€D by...

no you'll give them all the best that money buys

avert their eyes
from the rainclouds that are
gathering under superheated skies

teach them for the future
to make money their pleasure
though there may be no future
sold out to the now

In your scramble for security,
respectability,
personal equity,
you fail to see
your complicity

with the global system of brutality
and immorality
that money means to me.

What would you do for money?   *Kate Evans*

Part two - Fat gits in suits

Part three - Thinking outside the box

Presentation Two at the Management Skills Development Workshop of the Acme Packaging Company

Well, gentlemen
oh and of course
ladies -
I would like to begin
by reiterating our colleague's wise words
that a clear desk is indeed an efficient desk
but what I would like to talk to you about now
is the importance of thinking outside of the box.

I myself think outside of the box
for almost all of the time
and I would like to offer some thoughts
- thoughts, needless to say, from outside the box -
that will perhaps encourage all of us also
to think outside of the box.

Very well.
For ease of thinking outside of the box
it is useful to use a box that is smaller than your head.

If the box is larger than your head
(say if it is one of our standard single-wall low-cost
355 by 254 by 254 millimetre cartons)
there is always the temptation to put your head inside of it
and thus succumb once more
to thinking inside of the box.

Personally, I use our popular line
the little 50 by 50 by 70 millimetre presentation box
in 500 micron white box-board
which in addition to its suitable size
also neatly folds flat
for travel between home and the office
thus enabling me to think outside of the box
at home as well as work.

But thinking outside of the box
is not something that is done
purely for its own sake.
Thinking outside of the box
is above all important
in helping you to push the envelope.

And when you are pushing the envelope
it is well to use an envelope
that is rugged enough to stand the pushing!

In my case I use one of our excellent
280 by 240 millimetre manila envelopes
in strong 120gsm paper with 450gsm board backing
and pre-printed with PLEASE DO NOT BEND.

By placing the box centrally on my desktop
it is possible to push the envelope
outside of the box
in a potentially endless circular motion.

This of course is possible only
if you have kept your desktop scrupulously clear
on which subject I would remind you
of our previous colleague's sound advice.

As a final note, let me add that because
the unfolded and flattened dimensions of the box
outside of which you have been thinking
are approximately 230 by 100 millimetres
the envelope you have been pushing
(being 280 by 240 millimetres)
is the ideal size for flatpacking the box
so that it does not become scuffed, creased or foxed
in transit between home and office
and thus avoids the inconvenient and wasteful need
to constantly renew the box
outside of which you are now thinking.

Thankyou.

David Bateman

Corporate College

So, in fulfilling my mission statement
I re-prioritised utilisation of client and learner
services within an implemented provision of a
cross-fertilisation of disparate subject modules
alongside a fully semesterised and integrated
academic and vocational core curricula with
of course

accredited prior learning as an integral
and self-generating developmental part of
core competencies and quantifiable and
non-arbitrary criteria of resource-based
parameters as well as the creation of embedded
educational packages to stimulate potential
client awareness and thus needless to say

encouraging student-centred assimilation of
significantly relevant conceptual bridges to the
fulfillment of future career opportunities with
individual feedback up from proactive
involvement in meaningfully ongoing
tactile map progressions delivered by the
facilitation of consultative support mechanisms.

You mean?

Yeah, I taught 'em good, Dave.

Ken Champion

Financial Affairs

We were merely exchanging stock.
Love really clearly came as a shock.
I said: "If you feel like I feel,
I think we should go for a business deal."

She suggested that I urge her.
I tried the take-over bit.
She said: "You sexist shit!
I meant a merger."

I said: "No way, our kid,
When I'm right on the verge of
A major bid for you."

All I wanted was the company.
But whooo! True passion'll
Take you over like a multinational.

She said: "You're too late, mate,
If you're mid-way through,
Cos I've already done what you plan to do,
Meaning I've put in my bid for you.

And I just spoke to my broker.
I've got controlling shares
In you and your heirs
In perpetuity…
So it's you that belongs to me."

All I wanted was the company.
But whooo! True passion'll
Take you over like a multinational,
Strip your assets and strip your cash'n'all..

She said: "Down on one knee!
Say those three little words to me."
I said: "Which three?" She said: "Think!"

I said: "Well now, let me see...
Hmmm... I know! Rio Tinto Zinc."
Well, she went frantic.
She'd never heard anything so romantic.

Woah! True passion'll
Take you over like a multinational.
All I wanted was the company.
But whooo! True passion'll
Turn you irrational,
Make you brash'n'll
Take you over
Take you over
Take you over like a multinational.

Nick Toczek

www.startuppoem.com

This next poem is a start-up poem
you can read it quietly or shout it
Please refer to your brochures for the sales figures
while I tell you all about it:

Startup Poem is a young but dynamic outfit
With a small but dedicated workforce,
and of course key intellectual property
which could place it as the top horse
in the ever more competitive race to capture
the international poetry mind share / audience rapture marketplace-thing

seriously dude - we believe that..

Startup Poem was originally spun out
of a wrung out strung out genuine poet who brung it out of his
  bona fide english degree at the age of 23
and as CEP (chief executive poet)
  now oversees the day to day leadership necessary to grow it
into a thriving knowledge based enterprise.
He maintains creative responsibilities for lies and truth
providing the creative juices and managing verse forms from haiku to sonnet,
as well as the marketing:
"You want lyrical delivery? - we're on it."

Startup Poem guarantees customer fulfillment within 3 minutes
via our winning state-of-the art communications
such as professionally constructed beginnings,
dramatic pauses,

internal rhyme and novel sentence structures
in syncopated time
all of which can be implemented without disruption
online
using the latest
slam poetry 2.0 platform

This poem is SPONSORED by...

I'm serious dude - it rocks.

Key proprietary technology,
held by the Startup Poem company
enables enhanced audience participatory brand recognition
and transnational protection
   allowing user restrictions
to be imposed via US, European and WIPO patents
   lodged in 118 countries
all disclosed and available for inspection
if you just make an application to view.

but before you do

   "Please note the words 'startup' and 'poem' in any combination are
trademarked at the US Patent office and their use and reproduction
is controlled, tracked, all rights and privileges intact, under the
safe harbour provisions of the bayh dole act"

- whatever the hell that is...

Startup Poem offers attractive licensing options for those wishing to
use the words
startup® and poem® and startup poem® patented literary
techniques

- In return we will license you a unique brand image, more up to
date and chic than your regular poetry slate.

Forward looking statements state:

In order to meet our projected growth rates we began
this year to implement a straight-forward
   neuroscan licensing pricing plan
   charging just one dollar per child, woman and man
whenever the words "startup" or "poem" are uttered
either aloud or in your head

This is enabled via a profit-sharing agreement with major publishers
who have embedded

neuro sensors in every page recording
which words have been read and then charging
your credit card as instructed

  so far this poem has cost you 26 dollars
Your account has now been deducted.

incidentally,
referring to Startup Poem enthusiastically
(in a conversational mention)
does not breach trademarks, patents or copyright
   - there's a special exemption.

Startup poem will be making its initial poetic offering (IPO)
via the information superhighway
- so I encourage you to go
to www.startuppoem.com where you can buy a
piece of this exciting new poem by logging on as an investor
Indeed you will notice that another joint-venture
with google adwords is already bringing in revenue faster
than I can can say 'shareholder value'

  This should not be surprising
at startup poem we are committed to finding
every means of monetarising poetry
and exploiting the rising value of language as an important currency
  in todays burgeoning knowledge economy.

Thank you, I understand that is all the time I get
my presentation is over. The share price is currently set
at 9.8 and rising - of course the marketplace is the ultimate test
if you believe as we do that poetry has a future
please do clap, whoop, holler, cheer and the rest
but most of all, dear reader
  I encourage you to invest.

Jim Thomas

This poem is SPONSORED by...

If (rebranded)

If you can keep your trade when all about you
Say that fashion's moving away from you,
If you can trust yourself when shoppers doubt you
And make allowances for their doubting too,
If you can move and not be boxed by product
If being lied about then deal in lies,
Or being deconstructed then deconstruct,
Ensuring it looks good, and O, so wise...

If you can dream and turn your dreams to profit,
If you can think outside the box again,
If you can convince the folk in your office,
And everyone in the public domain,
If you can bear to hear the lies you've spoken
Believed and turned into a lifestyle choice,
Or watch your ethos become a blank slogan,
And stoop, and recreate its worn-out voice...

If you can strip away at all the excess
And break yourself down to a five-word phrase,
And turn your mission statement into success
By convincing a journalist at Dazed,
If you can turn spreadsheets to posterity,
Make Powerpoint serve you after you're gone,
And make your ego look like sincerity
Get your name mentioned on Radio One...

If you can talk with illusion of virtue
Live in a penthouse and still say you're "street".
Be something that poor and rich can buy into,
Be something they wear, live in and eat,
If you can fill the unforgiving minute
With ninety seconds of distance run,
Yours is the market, and all the cash in it
And, which is more, you'll be a brand, my son!

Luke Wright

For those in peril in the City

Global Father, prudent yet,
Who underwrites the national debt,
Who bidst the gilts and shares to fall
And rise at thy all-loving call:
  O hear us when our spirit yearns
  To increase funds and boost returns

Oh Christ, whose talents go to him
Who buys his bonds for seraphim,
Who walkst upon the market floor
And goes for growth for ever more.
  O hear us when we bring our aid
  To those who have their millions made.

O Holy Spirit, who dost charge
A fair percentage and a large,
Who broods upon the City's fate
And grants us all the true base rate,
  O hear us when we boo those claques
  Who still applaud increase of tax.

O Trinity in Heaven and earth,
Maintain our value and our worth,
Invest in us thy children dear
Throughout the full financial year.
  Guard us all where'er we go,
  And balance our portfolio.

Josh Ekroy

I have decided

In view of continuing
problems and shortfalls

in the light of repeated
errors and delays

and as part of ongoing
improvements in services

I have decided

to privatise my eyes
to sell off my legs
to merge my brain and my arse

and review the position of my ears
extending their contract
in the light of performance.

Alistair Noon

Exit strategy

In company bonding sessions in London Dungeon
on dry ski-slopes and in dutiful shouting pubs
at enforced fancy dress parties

(forgive my jobbing glass of water
forgive my refusal of the peanut
forgive my flabby sunless mask)

on the learning curve I have discovered that
he who would come on board must play squash
and submerge himself in the project ethos

identify with it in the long nothing
and remember it in the moments of terror
the procedures of shark women

the insane importance the looped spectacles
the darkening eye reflected in the screen
my Quark Express is quirkiness itself

(forgive me my odd socks
my child's whooping cough
my parental clock in the afternoons)

the checking of dread lists the blurring of deadlines
the hugging of clipboards the putting to bed by Friday
the two-line e-mail that finds most grievous fault

the necessary bollocking by fax the need for a niggling text
the juggling of words in the earpiece
the flagging of messages the jagged edges

on the graph the trigger for the appraisal
my failure to meet targets the shortfall

(forgive my lack of proaction
my gestural teamwork

my non-interaction with strategic partners

and whatever was said about my listening skills)
my progress reports must be read backwards
my steering group has wrestled the wheel from my grip

the implementation of non-water-tight action plans
is not a viable option as of now
stakeholders want an even keel

business support organisations think
my communication skills could be worked on

(forgive my rampant unsustainability)

my brimming ring-binder is in need of development
my lever arch files are trimly gummed with self-adhesive fear
my core belief in the marketplace is rotten but

my nuisance value is infinite

it has its own brand of inutility which
identifies with the company product
forgive my out of line update but

I think we can trial it package it market it
run it up the flagpole and see who froths at the mouth
even if it's only the C2s who will be as greedy as ever
to be poisoned by it

forgive my desire for forgiveness
forget me for you know you will have to let me go

I pray no longer to your logo   Let me go

for I am outcome-focussed now.

Josh Ekroy

Part three - Thinking outside the box   44

Part four - Advertising will eat the world

Flogging tat

designer jeans filled with rips
shirts that look like acid trips
the kind of art you find in skips
Elvis dolls with podgy hips
crackers with no crack inside
beds without the legs supplied
puppies with an ugly side
nudism - the pocket guide
car alarms you want to hit
Nicorettes you cannot quit
torture racks to get you fit
talking Hobbits, talking shit
Argos rings disguised as bling
Slinkies that are lacking spring
Christmas trees that dance and sing
the greatest ever hits of Sting
newspapers with smudgy ink
stereos that go plink plink
Apple Macs that will not think
fake Hulks, coloured pink
vitamins that makes you sick
fast food that doesn't come so quick
boxing nuns on a stick
stuff a klepto wouldn't nick
Action Men with knackered feet
veggie burgers made of meat
jigsaws God could not complete
and a battery-powered parakeet
there's his'n'hers this'n'that
some that split, some that splat
the shopping mall is where it's at
one job lot - flogging tat

Steve Tasane

Advertiser's dream

Your Pepsodent smile
And Noxzema complexion
Glow in the light.
G.E. bringing things to life

Your woollen sweater, washed in Zero
Skin So Soft, are you an Ivory girl?
I am impressed by your all temperature Cheer
The Tide's in and dirt is out
I love the Sprite in you.

You are a modern woman
With no static cling
And the freshness of Bounce
Oil of Olay you have kept me guessing
You are Pert 2 in 1.
The choice of a new generation of Bud men.
You were flat until you went fluffy.
Low fat, low calorie but all of the flavour
You have Oxycuted all of your blemishes
Now you sleep nights and stay calm
Doing the Skor ritual on Lightdays.
And I know that you come in an enviro-friendly
package because you care.
And that this relationship is cash back,
no money down for one year,
with double absorbency.

Jeffrey Mackie

excerpt from **The Occupation**

1a. "Select from the styling menus on this website to customize the dimensions of your dream Audi".
1b. Grandad followed the old rule of thumb by which you calculate the required size of the bicycle frame by subtracting ten inches from your inside leg measurement.

2a. "The Audi Space Frame (ASF) took ten years to develop, employing 40 new patents, 7 new aircraft-grade aluminium alloys, and numerous new designs, production techniques, and super computer programs".
2b. Grandad assembled his bike out of spare parts in the garden shed, one Saturday afternoon. Total cost: 15 shillings and ninepence (including puncture repair kit).

3a. "Seating in the A8 is strictly first class. Audi developed a new organically tanned Nappa leather for the A8 that was designed for a smooth, supple feel with a breathable open-pore structure".
3b. Grandad softened the leather-top saddle (which was not organically tanned) with an application of dubbin purchased in a sixpenny tin from Woolworths.

4a. "Driver and front passenger seats come with 14-way adjustable power seats. A new remote activates four driver's seat memory settings".
4b. Grandad used an army-issue spanner (cost: one shilling) and his arms to raise or lower the saddle or adjust the tilt of its peak.

5a. "Designed to work specifically with the A8's acoustic properties and space, the Bose® Music System delivers acoustically accurate music reproduction at each seating position through strategic placement of eight high-quality loudspeakers via a 200 watt, five channel amplifier".
5b. Grandad whistled.

This poem is SPONSORED by...

6a. "Both A8 versions come equipped with a fully automatic dual-zone climate control system that offers independent temperature settings for the left and right sides".
6b. When it was cold out on the bike, Grandad wore his coat. If it got hot, he took it off.

7a. "Standard safety features include halogen ellipsoidal headlights with integrated foglights".
7b. Grandad clipped a battery-operated lamp to the front of the handlebars. The lamp had a dimming switch which enabled him to economise on battery use (batteries cost ninepence) by riding with a dim light when street lighting made a stronger beam unnecessary.

8a. "The optional warm weather package includes an electric shade for windows".
8b. If the sun got too bright, Grandad pulled down the peak of his cap.

9a. "Audi's 4.2 liter, DOHC aluminium alloy, 32-valve V8 engine produces 300 horsepower at 6000 revolutions per minute. Use of a variable intake manifold helps give the 4.2 V8 exceptional pulling strength at all speeds, creating 295 pounds of torque at just 3300 rpm. From a standing start, this advanced engine propels the A8 to 60 miles per hour in just 6.9 seconds".
9b. Grandad always said there's no need to hurry. Learn to "ankle" - the hallmark of a good cyclist. Drop the heel as the pedal nears the top of its stroke, so as to push it over dead centre, and drop the toe as the pedal nears the bottom of its stroke, so as to "claw" it over bottom dead-centre.

Paul Maltby

Advertising will eat the world

William Sieghart likes poetry. He sponsors poetry competitions which help some poets, even if many of us don't like poetry beauty contests.
But the day after May Day this year, William sent me a 'rare poetry commission opportunity. A leading advertising agency would like to use poetry in a forthcoming advertising campaign for one of its clients. As a result I am helping them to commission poems from poets.' Each poet will be paid £200. Up to £3,000 will be paid to authors of the 24 poems used in TV and radio adverts. What sort of poems? Well, the adverts are aimed at the 45-60 age group. 'They are adverts, so although very different from normal commercial break fodder the poetry needs to be relatively upbeat, conversational, witty, and thought-provoking. The main criterion is that the poems should give a sense of complicity and should make the listener feel understood.' And so on.
Why does this matter a damn? Because poetry is one of the few places in our civilisation where you expect the truth. And advertising is (very well paid) prostitution. So I wrote to William:

>art is the desperate search
>for truth and beauty
>   a matter of life and death
>
>   advertising is the cynical hunt
>   for maximum profit
>   a matter of lies for money
>
>   poetry makes love with the language
>   advertising rapes the language
>
>   music dances with children and gives them wings
>   advertising steals from children and artists
>   art is the opposite of advertising
>
>   poetry just ran to me
>   she is weeping on my shoulder
>   she is hurt to be in the same poem as advertising
>   'Get rid of them,' she whispers to me,
>   'Send those fucking advertisers away.'

yours sincerely,
Adrian Mitchell, Shadow Poet Laureate
PS: I hope no poets collaborate with your mistaken scheme.

On not taking up the agency's offer

Jonah says this world's a simple act,
a remunerative package, no devil's pact;
that cutting, pasting and setting size
don't *have* to mean compromise.

Deep in the belly I can hear the seas,
takeovers, turnovers overtaking GDPs.
Enzymes digest me, part by part:
first God, then politics, now art.

Alistair Noon

Selling out

remember the rock song
that shook
your teenage years

you danced alone
in your room; or
you went to concerts
with friends.

a loner or head of the gang,
it was yours

now you're thirty
and you turn on
the television set

and you hear the song
and think of your youth.

and you marvel at the
integrity of your heroes
who let the song
be re-written to sell
fun cheeze to kids

and you question
your own sense of direction
- the next decade
is yours.

Christian Zorka

Hype

There's a sale next week, I heard:
forty percent off words
little ones an even better deal
three for just a buck
    fun fat wow
what a steal, who could say no.

They'll throw in an *at* or an *on* for free,
if you mention the sponsor's name, add
a *this* or a *that* as a one-time bonus. Even
the big words have finally been marked down
pomposity, flamboyant, extraterrestrial
slashed to half-price, all those letters barely used,
no broken bits of syllables, fully loaded, each complete
with shaded nuance, innuendo, its own
derivations. Heck,
    the guy said that they'd sweeten
    up the deal: throw in
    a set of freshly-cut
    pronunciation keys.

Heidi Greco

Pioneers, O Pioneers!

Guns before Butter!
Strength through joy!
    Knockout slogans.

SS lightning bolts!
Swastika armbands!
    Stunning logos.

Hitler and Goebbels!
    Brilliant admen.

Adrian Mitchell

Memo to Barbie: Re the breakup

"Memo to Barbie" commemorates the (U.S.) Mattel Corporation's February 2004 announcement that Barbie and Ken are no longer a couple.

1. Let us make the announcement. Let us explain that you and Ken will always be good friends. Let us suggest that his replacement is waiting in the wings. Say nothing about the situation to anyone.

2. Prepare for jokes about mid-life crises and the "perfect plastic couple" - how the bridal gown is yellowing in your closet, how Ken doesn't have the equipment, how he's worn more costumes than the Village People, how the sex tape must have proved too much. Be ready for crude remarks about Chuckie, the Power Rangers, GI Joe, and trolls. Smile and say nothing.

3. Prepare for the moral outrage of those who don't like change: "she's failed as a role model," "separation shouldn't be a publicity stunt," "I remember when Barbie meant something," "isn't one Britney enough?" Do not address such comments. Do not defend yourself.

4. Get a makeover. Recall that you first won hearts in a swimsuit, and tell yourself you can do it again. Think California. Think beach bunny. Find the tiniest bikini top possible. Smile sunnily during the photo shoots.

5. Start selling yourself. Bring in the money, now. Remember what you owe us: we made you, we own you, there are younger ones dying to take your place. Don't tell us you're tired. Get out there and do your job. Think profits. Think performance. Think it's your last chance, Bitch.

Janis Butler Holm

Part five - Television will not be Revolutionised

Television will not be Revolutionised

T.V. is evolving. Is yours? - B.B.C

*Television: The drug of the nation,
breeding ignorance and feeding radiation
- The Disposable Heroes of Hiphoprisy*

You will not be able to leave home.
Big Brother.
You will not be able
To democratically elect
The next cabinet
From the comfort
Of your armchair.

You will
Be able to
Plug in,
Turn on and
Cop out

Because

Television will not be revolutionised.

Television will not be revolutionised,
Television will not be brought to you
By the British Broadcasting Co-operative,
Or Independent-Vested-Interest-Free-T.V.

There will be
No real participation
In the programming of this democracy,
No proportional representation

For those who don't hold
Big enough company
Shares to
Influence
Policy
Or who don't possess
An Oxbridge degree
(But still loyally pay
Their licence fee)

Because

Television will not be Revolutionised.

Television will not
Make life taste better.
Television will not
Drive your imagination.
Television is not
Designed to make a difference or
Built to last.

It will not make you
Love the skin you're in,
Breathe deep
Sleep tight
Feel more thin
Or make everyone a winner
Baby.

This poem is SPONSORED by...

You are not worth it.

Because

Television will not be revolutionised.

Television will not bring you
The news,
Live,
24 hours,
Guaranteed free
From the sort of
Language that colours
Your views,
Unbiased by the
Men at the top
Who get paid
Their dues
For towing
Whichever party
Line they believe
Will increase
The revenues.

There will be no pictures of protestors
Peacefully prostrate
in the middle of the road

There will be no pictures of protestors
Peacefully prostrate
in the middle of the road

Only black balaclava-clad bloc-heads
Throwing bricks through the windows
of Starbucks and
McDonalds
Because

Television will not be Revolutionised.
Television will not
Bring out the star in you.
Television will not
Make every little help.
Television will never admit
That when it encourages you to 'Live It'
What it really means is 'Buy It'.

It will not help you stick to that diet,
That delicious, nutritious show
For breakfast, one for lunch
And a TV dinner in the evening
Will not leave you loving it,
But rather reaching
For the bucket

Because

Television will not be revolutionised.

Television will not bring you
Judith Chalmers on holiday,
Snorkelling through decaying
Reefs bleached deep
From sea temperature
Increase caused
In part by the
Emissions released
By holiday-makers
Eager to test the
Truth of those transmissions
That promise a piece
Of a paradise quickly
Becoming deceased
Because

Television will not be revolutionised.

Part five - Television will not be Revolutionised   **56**

Television is not proud to be different.
Television will not make you challenge everything.
Television will not give you extra energy when you need it most.

It will not go further so that you don't have to,
Do the small things that make a big difference,
Or provide quality that speaks for itself.

Your happiness does not love television.

Because

Television will not be revolutionised.

Television will not show you David Attenborough
Neatly sidestepping mass graves in the Congo
Or pulling focus from
Displaced tribes
In the Serengeti
As he perpetuates
The myth of
Pristine wilderness,
Allowing you to see,
With hushed tones,
The velocity of the gorilla
The ferocity of the lion,
Edited
And with added-in soundtrack
To increase the level
At which they appear
To interact

Because

Television will not be revolutionised.

And as your satellite dish makes way for
Your cable connection makes way for
Your digital set top box
And channels proliferate
Like rabbits reproducing recklessly
For fear of being caught
By a 20th Century Fox
The number of flops
Will rise exponentially
To the number of new slots
And the revolution that promises
More of what you want to watch
Will prove about as meaningful
As the revolution that offers
Over a hundred flavoured vodka shots

Because television will always be television
Will always be television
Will always be television
Will always be television
Will always be television
Will always be television

Switch it off.

Ben Mellor

The Bible according to Rupert Murdoch

In the beginning was the Word, and the Word was Gotcha! And the Lord Rupert said let there be a Royal Family, and let enormous quantities of trivia and drivel be written about them, yea even unto the point where a mentally subnormal yak couldn't possibly find it interesting any more, and let babies be born unto this Royal Family, and let the huge swathes of nauseating sludge written about them surpass even that written about their parents, even though these babies and their parents are about as interesting as a wet afternoon on the terraces at Selhurst Park.

And the Lord Rupert said let there be soap operas, and let each of these soap operas be so mind-numbingly moronic as to make a wet afternoon at Selhurst Park seem a truly uplifting experience, and let entire forests and the ecological balance of several continents be destroyed in the endless vistas of retarded outpourings about these unspeakable transmissions.

And let there be enormous breasts, and endless bonking, and hours and days and weeks and months and years of chauvinistic right-wing propaganda so that the brain-dead prats who like the bonking and the soap operas and the breasts and the royal stories get the politics as well.

And let any journalist who tries to stand up to the proprietor and editor in the name of truth, and intelligence, and integrity, and journalistic standards, be summarily dismissed, and cast forever into a bottomless pit of decomposing chimpanzee smegma, and let those journalists who suffer this fate rejoice at the great career move they have just made.

And the Lord Rupert looked at his work, and even he saw that it was a load of crap, but this was the enterprise culture and it sold millions so it was good. And on the same basis he decided to take over the television too, and the earth itself wept, and little robins vomited, and cuddly furry animals threw themselves under trains, and the whole thing was filmed by Sky Channel for a horror nature programme, and the most awful thing of all was that this was just the beginning...

Attila the Stockbroker

Potato

6 o'clock. The newsreader
yanks off his tie, leans
forward from the screen,
and stuffs the material
down my throat.

He doesn't want to hear
about the day I've had.

The raw silk squeaks
between my grinding teeth.
I suck on his makeup and sweat.

He removes his shirt and vest.
One chrome nipple
on a blank chest.
He wants me to suckle

but I can't sit up. My ears
are full of potatoes, in sacks.
My head slumps onto the sofa.
I hear only the muffle of hessian.

Outside nothing happens.
The newsman's mouth chews air.
He sneezes. Blood
sprays on the autocue.

I want to bleach the screen,
soak it in white noise.
Rinse off the human limbs
that slide, dripping, down the glass.

In a minute,
the man will give us the forecast.

I fumble the remote,
my fingers turnips.

The headlines are peelings,
kitchen waste to be swallowed.
I low on the couch like a farm animal,
wallowing in the trough.

Rosemary Harris

That movie was so to die for

Suck the lights down:
landscape of molested Barbie Dolls
tarred and feathered and taught to sing,
and gymed men chesting with lobotomized anger,
all dancing around a plot's pinwheel, pastiched
from art genres and processed through focus groups
to generate pornography.

Desire extracted from hope and secured in test tubes
is mixed to combust as images on a screen
and concludes with four people dead and one young woman
staring into the distance in a five-thousand-dollar pantsuit.

In the dawn erased of all you know
roll the credits of all you are not.
Inhaled like a mushroom cloud
the film dissipates, and you exit the theatre
to a dinner of tining forks and laughter buried
by a procession of beer
arriving from the bar
translucent as holy candles
refracted in thick glass. Exterminate yourself.

Gregg Mosson

Part six - This land is not your land

On not being beholden to random investors

if something
is being
privatized

and i am not
the private who
comes to own it

whereas before
i was part of
the public
who owned it

then surely
i am being
burglarized

Christian Zorka

This land's not your land

A Republican Party Protest Song
By a global village idiot called Backwoodsy Guthrie

This land's not your land,
   this land is our land
From Columbus, Ohio to the
   Florida swampland
From the corporate jungle to
   the redneck ranchland
This land was made by Fox TV
It's bible bashin' Disneyland
It's yippee-ai eye for an eye
It's faith, family and flag
God, guns and apple pie
This land belongs to cowboys
In stetsons, spurs 'n suits
We're the Wall Street, Wal-Mart Waltons
John-Boy, Jim-Bob, Jack-Boots
   In the Burger Kingdom of The Stupid
Stupid is as Stupid does
Forrest Gump is President
Yee-haw! He's one of us!
We're Starbuckin' bronco Marlboro' men
We're big chief swingin' dicks
It's John Wayne's world in Washington
We're the Capitol Hillbilly hicks
We don't read books, we do action
All-American wham bam ma'am!
Schwarzenegger Uber Alles!
Gimme five! Jean Claude Van Damme!

Rambo is not a poet
The French is arty-farty funks
We hate cheese surrender chimpanzees
We hate perverts, pansies, punks
'Cos them flip-flop pinko girly boys
Don't walk The American Way
The Dixie Chicks are Communists
SpongeBob SquarePants is gay
Hollywood is Satan's whorehouse
It's the Sodom 'n Gomorrah Motel
Route 666 to Tinseltown
Is the road to burnin' hell
We ride the hosanna highway
Saddle up our SUV
We got a two-ton tank 'n a
   ten-gallon hat
O-I-L spells victory
We're Team USA cheerleaders
Go! Go! Go! The Pentagon!
Shakin' 9/11 pompoms 24/7
Armageddon? Bring it on!
'Cos we're the evangelical vandals
Shit-kick, kick, kickin' down
   Mecca's door
Rainin' baptist bombs on Babylon
Behold their Shock 'n Awe!
We're pumpin' out Mohammed's diesel

This poem is SPONSORED by...

Fillin' up Christ's limousine
Hallelujah Halliburton!
Glory! Glory! Gasoline!
Got no time for risin' oceans,
Ozone layers or polar bears
Kyoto - is that a Japanese car?
It's gettin' hot in here - who cares?
We export Nike swoosh democracy
Handmade with Asian sweat
And golden arches of MacFreedom
Built on African debt
Charlie Darwin was a monkey boy
His science fiction's over
The Almighty made us, that's a fact
Way to go Jehovah!
The American Dream is born again
It's a big name brand New Deal
It's a holy roller Coca-Cola
Prozac Happy Meal
It's Britney Spears 'n Bud Lite beers
It's Super-Size 'n Super Bowl
It's Dunkin' Donuts on your mind
It's botox for your soul
We don't spare no cash for trailer
   trash
You gotta help yourself Jose
We wipe our ass with dollar-bills
Da-doo Enron-ron have a nice day
We're the bullet-head neo-conmen
We're the mob that franchise fear
Cat Stevens is an evil terrorist

Folk with beards ain't welcome here
We zip 'em up like chocolate oranges
Shackle, cage, interrogate
We protect Wild West values
Strip, abuse, humiliate
We don't murder unborn babies
We're pro-life NRA
We Kentucky fry death-row deadbeats
We're electric KKK
We're the Saxon sons of Uncle Sam
Our blood's red, white 'n blue
There ain't no black in the
   Stars 'n Stripes
It don't fly for Apache or Sioux
We have loosed the fateful lightning
Of our terrible swift sword
We're the Pentecostal patriots
Kick-butt and praise The Lord!
This land's not your land,
   this land is our land
From the buffalo Badlands to
   the cotton-pickin' Dixieland
From the Dust Bowl wasteland
   to the Presley Graceland
This land is Jesusland! Amen!

Elvis McGonagall

Part six - This land is not your land

Dreaming on empty

I am dreaming on empty
Working land faded from green
And remember my daughter
Raped of her childhood
To lose herself in this
   birthworkdeath
   birthworkdeath
   birthworkdeath
Cycle of Fair Trade promises
And sustainable futures
   still brown
   still dead
   still missing
   still unattainable...

Our cattle are bones in the backyard
   calcium deposits
   faded yellow
   gouged
   by ravenous teeth
Our hunger is bigger than our thirst for knowledge:
I forget to learn to write to defend myself
As I work the ground till my fingers bleed.

Don't understand
What the WTO is,
That somewhere animals fatten on food daily
What I feed my family weekly.
Don't understand
What they do behind closed doors
In resorts of palm trees and white sand
Speaking of my future
Trading promises like playing cards
When all I see is dust
Blow between straw houses.

Heather Taylor

Investment

They arrived all in black and silent,
starving from weeks in the jungle,
the lost whistle of malaria nights.
Crossing the border
that is carved in glass.

The note reads -
you have been informed.
Knowledge is murder.
Towers burnt to the ground,
the drilling of alien hearts.
The black blood of oil
fills your pockets.

It's such a long way to fall,
suicide by a swimming pool.
It's too much weight
to carry on one bowl of rice.
Your conscience light as a feather.

The station is full of porters.
Your suitcase holds whole forests.
The ghosts move on
combing their way through the shadows,
their eyes under house arrest,
their mouths sewn shut.

You pay for your girls in kilograms,
the cheapness of young flesh.
There are red lights flashing.
It's dangerous here at night
with the children carrying machine guns.
If you stroll across the minefields,
you will see how well your money is spent.

Aoife Mannix

My pen has a name

This poem is sponsored by

The people whose land
Was cleared for the mine
They, and others, then worked
And died in.

The people whose hands
Worked the crushers and smelters
They watch from their slum
In the cold dark.

The people who packed
And stacked up the ingots
In the holds of ships,
Then walk for their water.

The people whose land
And kin, they never see
As, from decks and cabins
They post their pittances.

The people whose hands
At lathes and presses
Turned out a pen, costing more
Than they own.

The People,
Whose names I will never know.

Spencer Cooke

The Oil and Gas University

I innovate and engineer. We form
New models, rejuvenate the fields.
The sectors interface. In Novosibirsk
She wears a hooded parka. She
Challenges outmoded ideas. She

Transforms the education-research
Manifold and provides new incentives.
Her name is a complex amalgam.
She pulls her hood back to reveal
A white face restructured by bone

So that beauty achieves real excellence
In a real-world setting. Her lips
Hit each of the seven key targets
Set by the national institute last year.
I record her and itemize the frozen rain

Which begins to fall on her impressive
Face. Ownership and exploitation
Have no place in this exciting dynamic.
Opportunity, however, is vital here
In this oil and gas region near the pole.

She walks past the infrastructure.
The gas flares in the fields, the tundra
Reciprocates under the white solar
Glare - then continuous darkness
Of course will eventually supplant this

Brilliant feat. High technology
Must provide a nexus and intensive
Inventories. She is beautiful and I
Wish to introduce myself to her
At the Oil and Gas University.

Todd Swift

These Gifts (ii)

For Bronwyn Lea

Let's begin with dawn. Not quite rosy red fingered
as in Homer's heyday, but blue, tinged with death.
The factory workers' early morning shift heroism
goes unnoticed. Even the birds aren't fucking yet.
Sunrise is the planet earth's clock-in card isn't it?
Emerald sparks fly as The Green Lantern scans them.
Bar-coded, human engines cough & turn over again.
On Merri Creek yellow mist drizzles like poison.
Turns gravy brown as it touches water, or mustard
even. Late heat bleached by chemical spill. Still no
work in Bhopal, as white-tailed black cockatoos tear
into silky oaks & shriek; fire alarms hunt casuals out
of their WMD's (Workplaces of Mass Dehumanisation).
Only a modern economy can sex it up & in the blink
of a lyric moment two butterflies have screwed each
other: gone for the kill. These gifts, I give them back.

B R Dionysius

Corporate Olympics

It was one of those moments when
The London sky just altered, in a flick from grey to blue
And after days of freezing blankness when
The East End streets slid dully under you
And drivers shivered in their steely cars
And local cats sat sullenly on sodden walls
The whole thing changed, like that
I was walking near the marshes, on the sports fields, at the time
Plodding over pitches in the unpoetic grime
Of what was due to be a coach park, or Olympic blocks of flats
And gazing at the Gherkin, and thinking well, that's that
They've held this place for centuries, this common piece of land
Still, nothing lasts forever, and whatever, things come round again
But as I turned resignedly, away from the designedly
Approaching blocks and towers, while shrugging at the flowers
The sky went blue, like that
And all the trees waved joyously, in golden light, in sun
And the roses all rioted, and small red houses smiled down on
The people coming out to hear
Their grass give out a vast green cheer
And all the concrete massed behind
And all its blacks and greys combined
Could not withstand this piece of land
We fight for local colour, with our flowers in our hands

T Troughton

Swimming hole

there's a hole that we used to swim in
half a mile northwest of baltimore.

the water was so bright blue
that no one could believe it was healthy to swim in.
(chemical runoff and whatnot).
an old quarry that had filled up with rain
and all around it piles of gravel
high as short mountains.

we'd climb up into them, into some nook
that blocked out the landscape just enough
that we couldn't see the ever-expanding
suburban developments to the north,
or the doomed trees to the west
and we could look up and see vultures watching us
rest in a manufactured desert.

now i hear they're making a mall there.
filling up that hole with water from somewhere else.
tearing down those trees
to make room for stores and ATMs and a fountain.

money is blood caked on a wall,
a reminder of that moment
suffering turned into value
and profit came from pain.

it's hard to find a good swimming hole
(what with the chemical runoff and)
bored cops out to bust naked people and
property owners and developers trading around
the commons like a dumptruck full of gold.

a friend leaned over to me on one of those gravel mountains.
"enjoy the good old days right now," she said
"because it only gets worse from here."

Mark Gunnery

River

How does water belong to the river
so when it rises above the bank
and floods the plain
we say
(as though it has colonized crops)

the river has flooded the fields;

and when light reflected from the river
streaks ribbon-leafed branches of a willow
is it the river
or the sun
who is responsible?

Janet Vickers

Monopoly

"...and after that the crumbling of the moon,
the soul remembering its loneliness
shudders in many cradles."
- from "The Phases of the Moon (Wild Swans at Coole)" - by William Butler Yeats

Here comes the crumbling of the moon;
like the bulb that's been held in the hand too long,
in the central office of the new sidereal real estate...

Stars for sale! Get your own personal piece of the heavens right here!
Name a star after your newborn babe!

In musical chairs, the chaos of turbulence slowly gathers
and someone's always left without a chair
until the last man sits triumphant all alone,
mid-world,
while the other players begin to disperse
drifting away to some new contest,
where, once again, they hope to win or acquire something.

Stars for sale!

Imagine - eternity for only a hundred dollars -
immortality for a song -

I've got your song right here:

I've got your star right here, his name is Upper Sphere,
and he can guarantee the time of year, can do, candu, this guy says the star can do...

This poem is SPONSORED by...

and the Little Red Hen is crying,
while the trolls snicker under the bridge
in the dark, dark waters of the greedy river

(somewhere down the greedy river)

and a few guys have all the hotels,
Marvin Gardens, Boardwalk, and Park Place,
and someone's sitting all alone
when the game is over,
on the sacred tree (of property)
whispering:

Stars for sale...don't be frail
Get your shiny new stars over here...

as he watches the moon crumbling
in the much too busy sky.

Cath Morris

Property

These silk petals lining the hedgerow,
a path past burning incense,
the offerings of Fanta bottles.
Barbie sat in her shrine,
her plastic face serene.
All the girls draped on bar stools,
their prayers no more nor less
than their beauty.
Their smiles are not for sale.
Only their bodies are patented,
the skin genetically modified.

A handful of beans,
the giant who lives in the clouds.
Such terrible loneliness
to want to own the world,
lay claim to the leaves themselves.
Inventing lies,
denying this other knowledge
that we are not streams of figures
on a screen,
but thousands of years of memory
held in water.

The healing secret of touch.
Such warmth cannot be found
in neon dollars,
the bed of a prostitute.
You won't be able
to afford my heart,
only the blood
pumping through it.

Aoife Mannix

Steal this poem

This poem is copyleft.
You're free to distribute it and diffuse it,
re-write it and abuse it,
and use it.
For your own ends,
and with your own ending.

This is an open source poem
entering the public domain.
Here's the source code,
add a little salt and pepper if you like,
share it out amongst your friends.

Because I didn't write this poem,
I moulded it,
picked the lines out of a skip as I was walking on over here
took used up fragments of leftover ideas,
and put them to use.

Think about it —
I can't tell you anything new.
In all these millennia of human existence
there can only be a few new ideas to be thought through.
So do we treat them like rare commodities?
Plunder arctic reserves for new ideas buried deep beneath the permafrost,
suffocate them with patent protection
and junk the rest?
Or do we re-use and recycle them?
Pile our public spaces high with shared ideas beyond anyone's imagining.

So I steal a verse here and a line there
a riff there and a rhyme there
pass it on around the circle,
roll it up
add a joke
here have a toke
does it get you high?

This poem is indebted to Gil Scott Heron, Abbie Hoffman, Jim Thomas
   and Sarah Jones
This poem is indebted to all the words I've read and the voices I've known
This poem is a community of intellect, yours and mine,
This poem is ripped off line after line after line

Because intellectual property is theft
and piracy is our only defence against the thought police.
The revolution
will be plagiarised!
The revolution will not happen if ideas are corporatised
So steal this poem
and use it
for your own ends
and with your own ending.

This poem is copyleft
all rights are reversed

Claire Fauset

An open letter to enclosure

The sun rises and falls,
Things live and die,
Carbon and water cycle,
Without names, sponsors or owners.

A rose, bought and sold, still smells as sweet,
A nightingale, bought and sold, still sings full throated,
A man, bought and sold, is a man for all that.
Time, without minutes and seconds, still flows.

They are not social constructs.
Ecology is not a social construct.
Freedom is not a social construct.
Life is not a social construct.
They are names for processes and states
That pre-date society,
And will predate it.

Sometimes, in response to what you do,
I may seem slow.
Maybe I am learning to think glacially,
Beneath a mile of ice
As a piece of coarse sand
That collected, collectively
Grinds mountains to moraine.

I may seem compliant.
Maybe I am learning to think virally,
As a fragment of life
Breathed in with vital air,
That replicates and prospers
At the host's expense.

I may seem a failure.
Maybe I don't think like you,
With names, sponsors and owners,
But with blue sky, out of the box.

Spencer Cooke

Part seven - Plastic man

Plastic man

I knew a man
who lived within
a disposable plastic Sainsbury's bin
bag.
The whole affair was very sad
he was a plastic man
he was a plastic man

A plastic man will last forever
with a plastic mac
in the clement weather
of an indoor shopping superstore,
no he never steps outside the door.
He's a lazy, hazy, instant gravy
polymer daisy plastic man
he's a plastic man

Plastic man loves to spend
on plastic goods that never end.
He's got a plastic car, a plastic life
a plastic lover and a plastic wife
he's a plastic man
he's a plastic man

Intercourse and Super Bowl,
does them both by remote control.
Loves to watch and eat the telly
loves to watch and eat the telly!?
believe me when you see his belly.
He's a rubbery, blubbery, not very cuddly
plastic man
he's a plastic man

This poem is SPON$OR€D by...

Wrapped in rubber he loves to dance.
Sweats inside his plastic pants.
Whips it up into a trance
of Narcissism's withering glance
(in the mirror on the wall
the mirror there sees it all)
a polymer dream infatuated
with a love that's squashed - and laminated
he's a plastic man
he's a plastic man

You can bend him back but he won't break.
He's a plastic man make no mistake.
Woodworm, mildew, dry-rot, rust,
have no fear of blue-eyed bugs.
Impervious to wear and tear
this man could last for a thousand years!
But just for fun - everyday
he seems to get - thrown away
he's a plastic man
he's a plastic man

Now in years to come, as time goes by,
and archaeologists scratch the veneer of lies
and everyone needs an oxygen pump
(in paradise by the rubbish dump)
perhaps they'll wonder upon their knees
who did wrap each slice of cheese?
And say with awe across the land:

Verily it was the plastic man

Mark Gwynne Jones

Seven signs of ageing

Here's seven signs of ageing five signs of problem hair
Stain-free deodorants and perfume scented air
As you crawl out of the rubble there's no need to despair
We've got it over here and soon you'll have it over there
You'll have seven signs of ageing five signs of problem hair
Stain-free deodorants and perfume scented air
And brand new bedroom units full of clothes you never wear
Till you're so drugged up on having you'll forget they're even there

Where you can make mistakes then sue someone else for free
A blame and cash in culture no win and there's no fee
While your country's bombing children to set their country free
Well someone has to suffer just as long as it's not me
And you'll get free toys from Disney if you feed your children shit
They can stuff their sorry faces until they've got the set
They can drink Coca Cola till they're as free as they can get
Till they're lazy and they're fat and they're no longer any threat
Then you can watch Madonna advertising Gap
While children sweat in sweatshops to bring you brandname crap
A brandname badge of honour to put you on the map
Just take my hand I'll take you there there'll be no turning back
And you'll get interest free credit with nought to pay till May
And more and more enticements to overspend your pay
Until you can't afford it and they take it all away
And you're drowning in your debt a little deeper every day

Then we'll give you religion to wash away your sin
Just open up your spirit and let the light flood in
It's easy and it's quick it does what it says on the tin
Just close your eyes then close your mind and put your faith in him
And you'll get life everlasting 'neath striped and starry skies
And the Cross of St George will rise up before your eyes
And this land of hope and glory will feed you bullshit spin and lies
Until one day you find your freedom fucked with freedom fries

And you'll have seven signs of ageing no-one ever saw
Five signs of problem hair you never had before
Till karaoke pop stars leave you screaming out for more
And you line up meek and mild as they lead you off to war
To save your seven signs of ageing five signs of problem hair
Stain-free deodorants and perfume scented air
And brand new bedroom units full of clothes you never wear
Till you're so drugged up on having you'll forget they're even there

And you'll sleep a little deeper each and every day
Till the starving and the homeless all just fade away
And you won't remember life could be any other way
And no-one ever listens to a single word you say

Philip Jeays

Cannibals of the western world

Like soft fruit, we're boxed up.
We're banged up and lidded.

We're stacked away, packed away,
Pre-taxed and gridded;

Apartmented, motorised,
Mortgaged and kiddied;

Each income computed
And suitably quidded.

Then citified, pitiful,
Puddled and giddied,

We're herded on wagons
And wheelied and skidded

And bundled to market
And monied and bidded

And cutted and gutted
And bloodied and ridded

And sliced up and eaten
And each of us did it.

We're animals.
We're the common herd.

We're the cannibals
Of the western world...

Cannibals
Of the western world...

Cannibals
Of the western world.

Nick Toczek

Excerpt from **KnockBack** *'The magazine for women who aren't silly bitches on a diet'*

Magazines for THOSE girls, fuuuuuuck you, it's official, YOU are my problem, with your shiny skin and your boho shirts, your straighteners and issues, £2.99 to shit on my ego is more than I can afford thanks. Fat or thin I've got places to be, and they are as far way from you as possible. You blow dry your hair for hours and cry at Disney films, you float about in flowers and twat on about nothing on your cell phones. You want me to worry about men and feel guilty about sex? Fuck you, I've been able to handle men for years, it's women who scare me and it's your fault because you've turned feminism into a war zone, you've created a monster and the monster is you.

I'm done with this shit out of you, I don't look like her or them or say that or hate myself for whatever you decide is out now, I don't have time. You patronise me with stories about plastic wankers in tinsel town and the issues you invent for them. You don't represent me or anything I think. You infiltrate the minds of the women around me and turn us into our own worst enemies. Pipe the fuck down about losing weight and instead give some column space to the fact that we have ambition, imagination, a sense of humour and something to say.

I hold you responsible for those scary fucking women out there, and for making me think I need to be like them to get by. You can't keep a good girl down, but you can die trying and fuck off while you do. You got it all wrong, and we've got other ideas. We don't read women's magazines, they're shit. We write KB, because fuck, someone had to.

Marie Berry

Dead Meat

if we are what we eat
then we are a super-sized enterprise
of burgers and fries
the globe's golden arch
enemy
restaurant chains that got the land on lock
branding the earth
enticing us to jump out the fire
into their frying pan

if we are what we eat
then we are a
high fructose corn syrup sipping
sorbate sucking
guar gum chewing
monoglyceride munching
assembly line of bleached flour
being paid under the kitchen table by the hour
the world's latest wonder since sliced bread

if we are what we eat
then we are designer beans
high fashion caffeinated manufacturing
fascists dictating the price of trade
making deals with the IMF
to keep our stocks from slipping
star bucks who once played in the NBA
now get paid to CEOkay our agenda to the masses
who sip hot Columbians for breakfast

if we are what we eat
then we are diabetes on a stick
cancer in a cone
a stroke to go
microwaveable bowls of irritable bowel syndrome

if we are what we eat
then we are a drug-infested body politic
over-priced pill-popping dope addicts
fiending for little plastic-coated rocks
provided by corporate dealers and M.D. pushers
smuggling everything from Ritalin to Viagra
across Canadian borders
pushing prescriptions
take 2 three times per day
so we can stay high
from the day we are born
to the day we die

if we are what we eat
then we are less than 5% of the world's population
who devour the rest
making them refugees
who we force-feed
with blind-folded taste-tests
the entrails of our waste
telling them it's a complimentary multinational breakfast
that comes with their stay
at the all-you-can-eat buffet
where we are the diners
and they are the main entree

if we are what we eat
then we are
foul fowl
crazed cattle
spilling spoiled milk spiked with steroids
into cartons being chugged in our schools
by hormone-raging kids
with diseased mouths and feet

if we are what we eat
then we are dead meat
dead meat
dead
meat

Ewuare X. Osayande

Ethical Consumer

My fair trade coffee is running out
My organic honey's run dry
I'm sick and tired of wheat free bread
It tastes of utter shite
Now, I don't buy Bacardi
They support US blockades
Against Cuba because of Castro
So I just drink cherryade
I don't buy Israeli produce
I think it should be banned
This food that is grown on stolen
Palestinian land
And I don't drink Coca Cola
It's far worse than it seems
It makes you fat, it rots your teeth
And funds corrupt regimes
But it's a nightmare in Waitrose
Shopping takes all day
While other women count the calories
I'm checking where it's made
My choices are quite limited
I never get a bargain
I miss the buy one get one frees
And always end up starving
But I'm an ethical consumer
And I walk the moral high-ground
But I'm feeling rather weak and faint
And need to have a lie down
I'm an ethical consumer
And I'm really on a mission
But I never eat three meals a day
and I'm getting malnutrition
So if you're after fast weight loss
Then comrades hear my call
Be an ethical consumer
And eat nothing
At all...

Sheena Salmon

Don't buy it

I've always been seen
As a little bit green
In my cosy, middle-class social scene
Ever since I made that lentil stew
For Abigail's birthday do,
Wore Birkenstock's to Brina's wedding
And got those rainforest patterns for the children's bedding.
My friends all think it's nonsense
But I'm proud to be their conscience;
Their commitment may be scanty
But my bottles of Chianti
Ride the back seat of the Mazda to the bottle bank at Asda,
And the second home in Rome has such amazing double glazing!

But that young fellow on Newsnight
Keeps talking 'bout the planet's plight
And I get a niggling feeling I'm not doing this quite right,
Driving to the protests in the seven-seater,
Discussing climate change under the patio heater.
I turn on Radio 4
It's "You and Yours"
(Which I adore)
But they're discussing what's in store
For the planet, with Jude Law,
Whose made some film about a war,
And then they interview Al Gore
And I realise in an instant that I should be doing more.

Thank goodness "In-Style" magazine
Has a special pull-out section: 20 tips on going green.
And it turns out the solution
To global destitution,
Exponential air pollution,
Endless wars of retribution,
Isn't global revolution,
Power devolution,
Wealth redistribution,

Part seven - Plastic man

Or the long-overdue reform of some of our fundamentally compromised
    international institutions;
Don't listen to "experts" who dare to proclaim
That our crazy mass consumption levels might just be to blame;
For everything you need to know
About economic justice, you can ask...Bono.
He knows the way out of this fix:
SHOPPING: it's the new politics!

To halt our mad rush to consume our blissful way to eco-doom,
To build a world not based on greed for things that we don't really need,
The answer is - you'll never guess -
We'll shop our way out of this mess!

Anyone who's got the gumption
Can do ethical consumption,
And thus turn the global tables
Buying things with pretty labels

So now all my silk pyjamas
Come with shots of smiling farmers.
Our sound system's been upgraded
But the box was fairly traded.
As I sit beside the hot tub to remove my sandals
I breathe the guilt-relieving perfume of organic scented candles...
They grew these pears with love and care, 5000 miles away
And I got these natural shampoos on the flight back from Bombay

The local shops are closing down
But there's no need to panic;
That big new Sainsbury's, out of town,
Does everything organic.

I've even managed to persuade my crazy uncle Rhys, he's
Using eco-friendly bullets now to hunt endangered species.

As for the global warming warnings,
Here's what I can do:
Plant a few plantations
For the carbon sequestration
(Based on flimsy calculations)
Strip the native vegetation,
Shift the local population
To some piece of desolation barely fit for habitation
And with misery and poverty "off-set" my CO_2.

* * *

Now, please don't think this poem's unfair;
I'm not saying it's wrong to care,
To think about the things you buy,
To ask who made them, how, and why;
But if you're promised cheap salvation,
Easy wealth for every nation,
An end to global poverty,
Avert climate catastrophe,
"It's easy - it will be enough
To simply buy more of our stuff!"
Don't buy it - try to understand
We need to change far more than just our washing powder brand.
The answers to our global woes
Won't be found with shiny logos on a special aisle at Tesco's.
We need to tackle head-on
Our rush to Consumageddon...
Leave the shopping in your trolley
And resist this global folly,
We'll fight back! - we'll all play a part,
There's much to do; but here's a start:

To keep humanity
On the map
Please, just stop buying
So much crap.

Danny Chivers

Book shopping

you know things are
wrong when
at the checkout
at barnes and nobles
you chose to pay cash
out of fear that
someone somewhere
is tracking the books
you're buying
for they have the right
to track that kind of thing
and the bookstores
have to obey
or risk sanctions
and history tells us
that when a law gives
rights to the government
they're certain
to make use of them
you're checking out
and you dig out a $10 bill
      and change
and pay
      and walk out
           knowing all the more

the price
of free speech
a little more determined
to fight for it
knowing that one day
they'll go too far
and that the final straw
will come
and even those you least
expect
        the least political
and the least interested
will crack
and revolt.

Christian Zorka

Part eight - Have a Job™

Have a Job™

Hey!
Did you really enjoy school?
Then you'll LOVE 'Having A Job™'!
Come on and 'Have A Job™'!
What else were you going to do with your life anyway?

Remember at school you LOVED the threat of disproportionate punishment if you didn't follow pointless rules?

You LOVED getting up on dark mornings to spend all day doing things that meant nothing to you!

How about having some clearly incompetent stupid ignorant authority figure taking out their personal neuroses by lording it over anyone and everyone they're in charge of?

Well, 'Having A Job™' gives you back ALL of these hideous soul-corroding factors but with MORE pressure, MORE stress and - most thrillingly-NO LEAVING EXAMS!

That's right!
When you 'Have A Job™' you'll be worked harder and harder
so you don't just give most of your waking hours to meaningless tasks,
but you'll be so stressed and so exhausted that most of your time outside your job will be spent recovering from it and preparing for more of the same!

Your only slight escape will be the daydreams you have about the things you'd do if you didn't 'Have A Job™'

Hey, don't forget that throughout this time - just like at school - YOU'LL have to dress like a mindless automaton!

Yes! When you start 'Having A Job™' you'll revel in a lifetime of watching the humanity being slowly drained out of you as the ever decreasing minutes, hours and days of your life wash away into months, years, decades spent doing something so crap they have to pay you to get you to do it.

They'll only let you out once you're too old and too frail to be any use any more

(if you don't die first, that is)

Merrick
Radio Savage Houndy Beastie

New Mills

I'm in the call centre rut
The curse of the young
Don't fall for it, kids
You're going to get stung
The wages are crap
But the outside pays worse
Once you're in you're committed
You won't be the first
To come in with ideas
This a stopgap, that's the image
Then you build roots
A lifestyle a mortgage
Can't afford to leave
Can't put your home at risk
A paycut's fine
Until payments get missed

So the bell rings
My eyes sting
Strip lights and dust
And I'm tapping out codes
Until I combust
If you don't like it,
You can go somewhere else
British Gas
First Direct
Same shite
Different bells

So what if I won't settle
Accept what I've got?
Does 80 rejections a year
Sound like a lot?
CSA means they think that
I've got no ambition
No degree means that
I've got something missing
Bottom of the pile
Try to smile
Keep my stats up
Keep filling out forms
One day I might get lucky

Penny Broadhurst

Then...

I had a dream...

that the lollipop lady
licked the white stripes
off a zebra
And painted the words '9 to 5'
on it

Then the zebra stood on its hind legs
and fucked her

                hard

Then she got run over by a bus

                real hard

Then a herd of zebras
charged towards me
I stood there
accepting my fate

I put my headset on,
answered the phone
and said "Good morning, Customer Contact Centre. How can I help you?"
with every thrust
(Women are great at multi-tasking)

I managed to get all the post done too.

Ebele Ajogbe

Daddy had a three year head cold

There you are:
vat jumpin
skin lumpen
turning red eyes into hot dinners
steel rods into pay cheques.

Doing your best chemical soup-step
in jeans and a concept
of risk versus circumstance -
keep up your dance daddy
keep up your dance.

Arms stay wide for balance
so if you trip-slip
you'll spread your wings
through that death dip
and fly fly
up out of your predicament.
Close your eyes -
and think of the flowers
mom will be sent.

Tie up your old boots tight
and sleep well tonight
so you can keep up your dance daddy
keep up your dance.

*So what happens
if I fall in there?*
A fair question.
Fair.

*Well Fred -
I'd take this pipe
and hit you hard over the head.
Better than the alternative.*

At least that way
We'd know for sure you were...

Take comfort and know
that all possibilities
are thought about
fought about
fucked about
and then chucked out.

Through the cyanide fog you've sussed it all out -
who reaps the rewards of your tiptoes -
who drives home with clear lungs, good credit, and a pink conscience -
who hands you a week's notice when you're too sick to work
and when you don't crawl back begging
thinks it's quaint that you're proud -
who asks you to swallow your tongue
and not let your doubts get too loud -
who punches every cost-saving
close shaving minute way past the limit
regardless of what the law allows -
who hands you a hard hat in the name of Health and Safety
and without a trace of irony tells you to be careful there mate -
who has no idea that your wife sits rigid and tight
every fucking night
breathing out only when you walk through the door
coughing, weeping, and late -
who's willing to take you from your family
for the sake of a little more money

just a little more -
honey -
and no prize for your grace
for the sweat on your face
for your strength in the place where you dance.

I still remember
when you used to dance.

Michelle Green

The Conference of the (underemployed) birds

"It shows the top half of the workforce enjoying permanent, well-paid, full-time jobs, while the bottom half can find only casual, poorly-paid, part-time work which, as Labour market economist Professor Sue Richardson warned this week, was creating a class of "excluded and dangerous" men with incomes too low to support a family." - The Age, October 04, 2003.

"My discourse is sans words, sans tongue, sans sound: understand it then, sans mind, sans ear." - Farid Ud-Din Attar, The Conference of the Birds

(i)

A Willy-Wagtails' call intercepts the morning. Birds were real once, like jobs.
The modem's dial-up scream is cut short; why is our technology suffering so?

Fake, Australian accents in the call centre aviary: Calcutta nest robbers gloat.
A taxidermy of outsourced work: ditto, we're all stuffed on the global floor.

Bottom of the bird market. This new flu's crashed like tech stocks, Acme trap
For the Roadrunner managerial class, the coyote - disenfranchised American?

(ii)

Magpies don't attack in the open anymore, have you noticed: phenomena?
Phone tab's the way forward. Keep an eye on your receiver, not the skies.

There are new powers afoot for dealing with these full employment refos,
Our government issues wide-brimmed hats with strings of corks attached.

The contemporary job market has a thin eggshell; depleted proteins crack.
An excluded & dangerous class birthed? They backed job terrorism not us.

Part eight - Have a Job™

(iii)

I saw a hoopoe once. Was it Jaipur? Its crown of truth strutted on the lawn,
Painted a post-colonial green. What good is spiritual knowledge without law?

You will play an integral role in this dynamic environment by fudging your
Work history for sure. Service orientate your brain - lively, world class, lame.

Dangerous as ideas? There's a metal storm inside your head. Try Sufism?
Was it John Lennon or Steve McQueen who went on about "ism ism ism?"

(iv)

There are nightingales here reputedly. Wasn't it someone from myth who
Couldn't stand being unemployed anymore & turned themselves into one?

Hit an epic glass ceiling probably. Better to be amorous than under-employed?
There's no new twist in the figures though. The virtual exclusion of women

From net growth in full-time job mythology is eons old. Sumerians started it.
Gilgamesh's entrapment of Enkidu needed a woman's art: 'Wanted Harlot.'

(v)

Australia has plenty of parrots, but cockatiels inhabit our universal currency
Of shame. See them locked up in Athens, Rome, Madrid, Delhi & Bangkok.

Feathered service economies, budgerigars tell beak fortunes in Iranian streets.
Collars of gold chained to human profit. Flocks flee drought & agricultural rut.

We even killed off one sub-species called 'Paradise', cleared full-time underbrush.
& if they were flightless, then we paid out redundancies see: dodo, auk & moa.

B. R. Dionysius

The Commuter's Song: 7/7, 9/11

all good children go to heaven...
I'm dying just don't get me started
bits falling off like kit at a party:
started with my eyes,
they saw it and went blind,

I nearly lost my mind
along with half my hair.
Came off worse than Tony Blair
nine years into a doctored tailspin
not looking any younger.

We are all soldiers on this bus
marching to our ordered work
It's not an innocent among us.
It's not a call. You can't shirk
the life you live, the shoes you wear

your hair, your jeans, the car you drive.
You do drive, don't you. I thought so.
Uniforms and business suits
pokemon rucksack looks real cute.
Kawaii!

Hand in hand with Mickey Rat
Chairman Mao and Uncle Joe
Google sections cyberspace
in the window I see your face
dissolve in the light fantastic.

Fandangled skies across the border,
sunrise on the new world order!
Television on demand,
mobile phones report our plans
digested by the smart machine

that broddles deep inside our dreams:
boxed, cocked, locked and loaded
a pair of Purdys pulling points
on Nectar cards:
easy money for our shills

trading on the unfulfilled,
loveless, luckless, buckless, fuckless
botox stuck, nipped, rolled and tucked,
lonely alcopop sensations
who sleepwalk backwards to the grave

overcome by simulation.
The more you spend the more you save!
... like wanking on your wedding night
you had the chance to get it right.

We are all soldiers on this bus
singing the end of history blues.
Arms and legs are funny shapes
that mould don't hold and merge in your back
as visceral as an Easter sheep

that's seen the jar of mint sauce. Confused?
I am abused by GATS, SATS, CAPs
and the ROI, unleaded futures,
MarComStats and microcaps,
angels from hell with nothing to sell

but money. There is nothing special
about this dying, you could do it too
without even trying. (Oh wait .... you are ....
how about that.) No rats to smell
I've gone to hell and there's no crawling

This poem is SPONSORED by...

back. In terms of beats we're all
a piece of the original mammal plan;
like the five-fingered hand and embryo fish
all our parts come down to this:
return to God, address unknown.

We are all soldiers on this bus,
marching for an easy life
piled high, sold cheap, discounted deep
so deep into the dealer's margin
the pips squeak, the stone bleeds,

the canary pirouettes in the cage;
my last days drift the vision fades,
'til something living reclaims my waste.
There's no one home and the lights gone out
there's no time left for it's my shout,

I'm dying just don't get me started
bits falling off like kit at a party,
not quite feeling hale and hearty;
doctor says its down to the bone,
my joint's unhinged and I'm all alone.

It's cold.

George Roberts

£8000/year ≥

eight thousand pounds a year
puts me in the richest twenty percent of people
on this rock we stand on
but here my hands are stuck
   on credit card hard plastic fears of not having
with the British Broadcasting Corporation
and it's less moneyed brain bend buddies
telling me to spend spend spend
buy myself some friends
from that bit at the end of the Weekend Guardian
well done well done
and thanks to the advent of hire purchase
and buy now - give us your liver later
we can all masturbate over Marks and Spencer
gourmet food fuck dispenser
*Because it's not just a grossly overpriced
cheese sandwich*
buy some more toys and triple skim soy latte
to stuff down into that soul crater
throw it up and away later
I've got nothing to say to the repo gladiator on the doorstep
except
no, I didn't forget to make the last payment
but the heat stopped
and away went the last bits of shrapnel between this roof
and an eviction order
and now that the border between me
and the interest free
is looking three, maybe four times thicker
   I'm thinking
you know that bumper sticker on your van
the one that says *My other car's a Porsche* -
it doesn't make me laugh the way it used to.

This poem is SPON$OR€D by...

My grandma lived on what she shared, traded and earned
learned not to ask for too much
or clutch onto what amounts to
    at the end of 95 years
a collection of things.
No recourse to a larger source of possible purchases and conditional sterling
she knows a thing or two about how to accrue a wealth of dignity
and for the one two three under her wing -
    make it work.
These days she can hardly hear
but my ear is open
I need her stories
of how to -
    give everything you have
    live with a fierce passion
    fill stomachs and minds
    leave greed behind
and how to be a human
on eight thousand pounds a year or less

Michelle Green

Part nine - Living in the Nonsensedrome

Seven sleepers

Like an eagle in its nest
You sleep among clouds and streams of wind
That flow strongly, chill your heart
Sleeping like a mythical being in a cave
For a thousand years, beside your shield and helmet
It would be comforting to think
That kind of sleep could be refreshing
And that one day you would be woken
By an unasked kiss on the cheek
From a maiden who could fit in your hand

When I was young I realised
There was only so much to go round
And that greed ensured poverty
At the other end of the world or street
That people are only satisfied with more
That community does not survive a free market
And politicians are windy debaters
With their trousers down around their ankles
Superheroes exist only on television
And God would not want to live here
Unless He had a return ticket home
Capitalism runs on oil and sweatshops
Threatening the slaves with starvation

If I had been one of the seven sleepers
I would wake up unshaven and grumpy
To this age of running faster and faster
Across the earth's face
Strapped to the front of an automobile
Driven on by the slavemaster
Who is driven on by his master the Pharaoh
Do you feel free? Do you believe the papers?
If so, they have done their job well

K Simpson

The long drive

1. The long drive

I wonder what the drive is. The license plate, the cannibal calliope, the rushing flash of flesh, flash of flesh. And nuts make trees sometimes, and sometimes seeds make grass. Because we're all a part of this carpet called life on earth, wall to wall whatever if there were any walls.

And I'd like to be a bomb, ticking and wound up in a pocket on the way to whatever. I count life out in cigarettes and sterile sperm, my city life, country life gone, gone, long gone and longing's never gonna get it back again. Because there's too much time piled up between here and there. Too much history, too much civilization, too much human behavior, windowpanes between me and the weather. A bubble boy at home among all the others of his kind, wondering what sort of bomb could ever take back the centuries before he was born, take back the witch trials, the conquistadores, the monks and hospitals, the ideas that kill, all the ideas that can kill.

Dead corporate officers fall tonight, their days crushed like beercans and old cars, their tailored cuffs dragging in mud the colour of old blood. This curse is for them. I am native to nothing nowhere and so I claim the earth as mine.

2. "I have no idea what I want ..."

I have no idea what I want
And so I have nothing.
Mount Saint Helen vents,
I know this
I know bombs in Baghdad
I know The Ring Of Power
I know peanut butter and banana
But I have no idea what I want
And so I have nothing.

How fortunate
All the people I see
Choosing, selecting, advancing,
Mating, breeding, working,
Eating, buying, driving
All toward something
A great tidal bore of
Uninformed striving
Constantly reinforcing itself
Reassuring its many various parts
With the soft comforts
Of conformity.

The ads await like
Sexy straitjackets
And people slip on that
Sense of belonging
Of achieving, of being
Available for just
Three easy instalments of
$9.99
While I dither,
I babble, I squabble
I move back and forth
Like a feverish shuttle
Like a bad UN diplomat
Like a mutating virus

I'm waiting for a message,
For a sign
Not necessarily from God
But from some supernatural
Source.
I'm waiting and waiting
And when it comes
At last I'll be seized by
Conviction.
At last I'll know what's up
At last I'll become
A fanatic
A murderer
Like everybody else.

Vincent Tinguely

Shoplifters recruitment drive

Aberdeen City Council commissioned local poets to write about various neglected trades and professions. They asked me to promote shop fitting but I think I misheard them...

Shoplifting shouldn't be
All skagheads, chavs and neds,
And crusties that look like me.
Shoplifting ought to be, equal opportunity
If you've got deep pockets but no money,
Apply today. Strike a blow for impartiality.

Help dispel the myth, that if you shoplift
You put up the prices for shoppers. Cobblers!
It's fat cat execs who put up the prices,
They're there to care, for their shareholders
Their customers can moulder,
I say enough is enough, so nick stuff
It ain't a chain store massacre.

To shoplift, no experience is necessary,
All you need is and eye for a bargain,
And an ability to run faster
Than frustrated little Hitlers in peaked caps.

But if shoplifting you want to enjoy,
Better ask me to be your decoy,
Cos security and CCTV
Will automatically follow me,
Leaving you free to nick, unnicked,
While I act a shifty clown
Niftily lifting bottles of whiskey
Then putting them back down.

This poem is SPON$ORED by...

Yes, let's go to Tesco, where every little helps, so help yourself.
And slack security, is one more reason to shop at Morrisons.
Oi Jamie! Half inching from Sainsbury's
Is what really makes life taste better.
And sticky fingers and a big jacket,
That's why mum's gone to Iceland. Nice one!
Don't wait for the January sales for a bargain from Next,
Get a hundred percent off selected items, the ones you select.
If you can cut the security label off of clothes,
Well they're going for a snip.

The rich should be robbed by the poor,
So get out there and chore,
Cos every item in every chain store
Is on special offer, so join me
And buy none, get one free
Buy none, get one free
Buy none, get one free.
Forget ASDA price, this is ASBO price,
Nice to steal you, to steal you nice!

Rapunzel Wizard

The Klepto Dance

if nicking's an art, you've got to look the part, put on your Sunday best
brush your hair, dress debonair, it pays well to invest
tip-toe by the security guy, then tap-dance on with grace
you need more flair than Fred Astaire, with a far less shifty face
so follow the squeal of my trolley wheels, study the line of my eye
cover my back, block that rack, don't let that camera spy
baskets swing, tills go ting, I cast a bashful glance
with fingers slick as a Beckham flick I'm doing the klepto dance
it's easy - with frisky itchy fingers
it's easy - dip dip dip
it's easy - quick, stick it in your pocket
it's easy

our thumping hearts put a bit of oompah into that in-store muzak
two-for-one won't shake my butt, but two-for-free might move it
having two left feet doesn't have to mean the moves I make are drastic
this supermarket super trooper trips the light fantastic
the way I groove just goes to prove it's not ants inside my pants
this kind of dance doesn't stand a chance of landing any government grants
but it's top of the list of the things I do to keep my glow enhanced
I must be on weird medicine - I'm doing the klepto dance
it's easy - with frisky itchy fingers
it's easy - dip dip dip
it's easy - quick, stick it in your pocket
it's easy

the glittering array that's on display has put me in a trance
my body can't help but help itself, I'm doing the klepto dance
the convex mirror catches me in a convoluted stance
I look a bit illegal cos I'm doing the klepto dance
the store detective's stalking me, it's a modern day romance
he'd like to slap his handcuffs on, I'm doing the klepto dance
it's easy - with frisky itchy fingers
it's easy - dip dip dip
it's easy - quick, stick it in your pocket
it's easy
cos we're doing the klepto, doing the klepto, doing the klepto dance!

Steve Tasane

Gotham begins

An under-door flicker from your Bat-signal
torch tells me you're awake and Batman
has already completed some mission
using his Batcycle and Batmobile.
I double-check I've packed
your Batman Begins nursery bag.

Your friend knows the golden arches
but struggles to recognise an 'm'.
While he shows off his latest set
of McDonald's collectable toys,
you'll talk about merchandise
from movies you're not old enough to see.

You tell me your ambition is to move
to Gotham and become Fighting Girl.

Emma Lee

Lost in live streaming

For Matthew

Having spent countless years sedentary in a central-heated box,
opening windows that radiated solely Cyberspace to his mind,
to new sites the young man had nonetheless navigated,
like bold Christopher Columbus.

Without a wetsuit, he'd surfed tsunami-sized searches,
finding Darien, wild-eyed as Pizarro's men;
had stormed firewalls,
hacked his way thorough networks
that make briars look child's play.
Viruses he'd also fought, of a virulence worse
than those that White Man brought the Natives;
and giant worms, fierce as George's dragon;
yet overload it was to his system,
one bright day,
to find fields unfolding before
each troubled slit of an eye.

From his car, he squinted at their chlorophylled intensity,
an elfin green whose vividness he'd forgotten
once upon a time he'd ever seen.
Then, booted up,
he strode out,
downloading himself steadily,
powered by solar radiance, his ears attuning
to the real-time chirrup and twitter of all the birds,
until a sudden soaring of a Skylark - its intense warp and trill -
soon became too much, was too exquisite a sound
for the hard drive,
crash,
shut-down of his mind.

Part nine - Living in the nonsensedrome

Nodding mutely at the creaming bride-buds of Elder,
he plodded on, assailed on all sides by the sheer forcefulness of Spring
let sprung - the rampance of the Gose-grass cleaving to his side,
swishing Nettles beside his knees, the up-thrust of Umbellifers;
brambles tugging at his trousers, fairy-ringing Bluebells
beneath Hawthorn's seductive pull and pluck.

Still, bravely this young man continued,
breathing heavily as exhausted
he stepped into the woods,
but there,
heading on the bear-strong tongues of Ramsons,
the final straw came quickly
as overpowered
he sprawled,
lay undone.

Now, lost in live streaming
as the brook rushes and gurgles incessantly over stones,
it all floods back - a boyhood buried in deepest Suffolk.
Yet as he sits there, it seems it's still too big a shock,
you see, Nature has never, ever looked so exotic
as here, right beneath
his grown-up
nose.

Helen Moore

Positive images of gherkins

I'm
abseiling
down the cone
of 30 St Mary Axe
in protest that it is not
erotic; it is obscenely vac
uous office space. This dis
appointing phallus is uncharged
with semen, no orgasms erupt here,
erection without climax. I'm got up as a
pickle in sexy khaki combat gear, to prom
ote positive pickle awareness, but my act is
sabotaged by hunks of Emmenthal edging slowly
down like yellow rain. I like to think we're canapés from
heaven, not proprietors' publicity. Where are the wine
waiters? (The Swiss don't export their wine. They know their
limits.) The cheese hunks' kneepushes and outward swing make
the perspex vibrate as we descend to the near-vertical. I look down
on the peering ragged blocks that are the City then stop doing that. I'm
too close up here to appreciate my shiny pointy missile, (Look no Hans
Blix) a poisonous   weapon in the armoury of   gilts and
           trusts that should   have been sanctioned in   stead of
aw   arded a prize, this   rocket, this reflecting and   refract
ing   in the glimmers that   edge through forbidding   cloud.
Now   buildings move on to   a misty future of their own   mak
ing so   that whatever's left be   hind's a candidate for dem   olit
ion. Hey! Let's get the wrecking   ball to the NatWest Tower,   and
now that   Moor House is newly   complete it must be redunda   nt.
What's not   being constructed is   being destroyed for all etern
ity even St   Paul's, whose dome   from here is refusing   firmly to
enter into a   "dialogue" with this   mammon's teat, in spite of
what the pund   its its claim. Instead, I'm   reminded Wren built his
leaden cupola as   an observatory to furth   er his astronomical
interests and the on   ly "dialogue" is with an   undiscovered heaven
of planets and stars.   Now, at this point, I can   hear only the harang
ue   at Hackney. I'm bur   sting acne on the face   of indifference that
low   ers on the dirt-poor,   council back-to-backs,   just a cocktail's
toss   away, there's no iron   y in this contrast, only   a striped
greed   guffawing over ancient   poverty, smart money   so gross it
looks as   if it will launch all finan   ciers to Mars because   there
isn't enou   gh space on earth for all   their dollars, the gherk   in in
the chipbag   down below being the   dolour on the street, the
belch in the   downdraft. With the   dealers gone to the moon,
will we be for   ever bouncing off this   side, a playground for
protest, a ship   of leapfrogging fools or   will it find a berth on
Uranus? As I am   led away, arrested for tres   pass, damage to prop
erty, publishing a false   instrument I do not regret   this journey.

Josh Ekroy

Part nine - Living in the nonsensedrome

The constitution of stars

the moon has moved
the birds are involved in civil war
taxation has stopped the reach of trees
into the blue identity of heaven
the nine models of evil justice
have resulted in uncolliding planets for whose
existence most of us must take someone's word
words have been elected kings
and dispensations handed out
to horse-traders, honest and dishonest
the president's sons and daughters
are now born into their future
with the desire that every part
of this constitution stick together
without falling apart

it is a community of the inconceivable
where preambles the age of elephants
snort in the water-holes
and beasts which might be buffaloes
sit solidly like numbered clauses
on this page of earth
children fight over wildflowers
and judges sit in caves to pronounce
'You have' and 'You have not'

if in your hand you carry a star
through this land and you see a person
who would like to take it from you
hurry away!
they have not had a breakfast of stars
they have not had a lunch of stars
nor stars for dinner
the moon might move
and birds may be engaged in insurrection
and although this is also a constitution
for the starless
from cradle to grave you do not meet
power makes this a constellation of stars
and they glitter no less because
bodies hang from the questing trees
two houses from the end of town it is dark

swinging, turning
the light bounces off their teeth

M T C Cronin

Part ten - Beyond the mall

Beyond the mall

There are places there are hills
They're not just called hills, they're really hills
There are places there are forests
Not like "Twelve Pines," but really forests
There are places where the birds sing
And you can hear the eagle call
I know they're out there
Somewhere beyond the mall

There are places there are rivers
Not surrounded by concrete, but living rivers
With fish in them and frogs and little tadpoles
With ducks and deer drinking by the sinkholes
There are places far away
The trees turn colors in the fall
I know they're out there
Somewhere beyond the mall

There are places you can see the sky
Not neon signs and billboards, but just the sky
There are places with dirt on the ground
Without the miles of asphalt, not a car around
Where on and in the soil
Good little critters crawl
I know they're out there
Somewhere beyond the mall

There are places like that, and things don't have to be like this
I mean not cosmetic changes, things really don't have to be like this
There are places where people know their neighborhood
Where people live there and they think that life is good
There are places like that
Somewhere on this spinning ball
I know they're out there
Somewhere beyond the mall

There are places that I know I've gotta find
Otherwise I will undoubtedly lose my mind
Otherwise I'll end up just like you
On Ritalin or Prozac or whatever things you do
I'm going where the water is blue
And the trees are so tall
I know they're out there
Somewhere beyond the mall

David Rovics

Bring down the garden-centres

Bring down, bring down the garden-centres -
centres of wickedness, seats of corruption.
They mass-produce twine
and put traditional waterbutt-makers and trug-makers out of production -
All of the social securities filled
with members of the Waterbutt-Makers' & Trug-Makers' Guild.

Bring down, bring down the garden-centres.

Remember when your local corner-shop
supplied all of your gardening needs?
Trugs on the top shelf, next to the humbugs and gobstoppers -
and we were happy, we were happy shoppers -
Children filling their pockets with packets of seeds
the minute the shopkeeper's back was turned -
"Mister, can you get us down that water-feature?"

Bring down, bring down the garden-centres.

Remember 1381?
Wat Tyler was a trug-maker by trade -
he only made tiles for a hobby, just for a bit of fun.
Emmeline Pankhurst made concrete tortoises -
there's millions of us, you see -
And when I'm throwing myself in front of a birdbath on Saturday,
where will you be?

Rachel Pantechnicon

Changing the world

If I were to write a book called, "Changing The World,"
It would have a recipe for chocolate cake
With instructions on inviting one hundred strangers around to taste it,
And make strong suggestions for getting their own favourite recipes in return.

It would have instructions on holding convocations of school children,
To ask them what would be the most appropriate punishments for parents who slap, snarl and beat,
And give instructions for Non Violent Direct Action
Where children can learn the tactics of naming and shaming,
Making banners, invading offices and using mobile phones to contact their lawyers.

I would instruct soap opera makers
To include story lines where Ken Barlow
Leads a radical faction of Amnesty International
In invading the local engineering works that manufacture torture instruments for use in America and China's prisons.
Ken would lead the group in smashing them with domestic hammers.
The Rovers Return would become a theme pub for homecoming revolutionaries.

I would give instructions on what presents to give your lawyer
After he has taken the Government to task for their latest misdemeanours,
Organic champagne, home grown strawberries and a favourite Chocolate cake recipe never go amiss.

My book, called, "Changing The World"
Would have poems, party games, origami instructions, paper aeroplane folding instructions,
And suggestions for successful tree planting.

I would give instructions on holding impromptu comedy festivals
Outside the houses of those that advocate flogging, hanging and the bringing back of the birch
To encourage community participation in the assessment of gentle mocking humour as a revolutionary tool.
I would encourage the melding of the work of Kenny Everett, Jennifer Saunders and the Goons
With the work of Marx, Engels, Goldman, Pankhurst and Tatchell.
"All humour to the Soviets," would be one of my chapter headings.
By writing my book
I might not feel that I was changing the world
But that I had encouraged a few dedicated and wonderful souls.

But instead I will sit in this cafe,
Drink tea,
And watch the world go by.
Oh look, over there, another handsome young man on a microscooter,
And over there I can just make out some stragglers from the latest riot outside the WTO talks.

How grand the world seems today.

John Hoggett

resist.pl

a computer program for resistance written in perl script

```perl
#!/usr/bin/perl
sub b($){1;}
sub is(){1;}

BEGIN{($thinking,$acting and $fighting);
        sleep $later if not kill $you, ($first, $the_powerful)}#...

uc(our $planet);is; not $machine and not $factory;
(our $planet)=($fragile, $delicate and $alive);
(our $lives)=($on=>'knife_edge');

uc(my $life);is; not $meant; for (@sale and
  $i_am){}; not $a{"demographic"} or $a{"market segment"};
$i_will; not $lie_back and $let_you; kill $people for ($profit);

$corporate_masters='power, guns, influence';

$fight; while(<we_can>)
   {$live{'free'} or die 'trying';}

for ($love){};
for ($anger){};
for ($fun){};
for ($fucks_sake)
   {$stand_up &b $counted; join $the, @resistance };

our $planet=>is_being_slowly_strangled;

until ($planet=>belongs=>(2*(each %person)) and not $corporate_masters){
   not $Shell; not $Esso; not ($BAE or $Halliburton);
   (our $lives);not $viable;
   not (our $species); last;
}
```

Part ten - Beyond the Mall   126

```
$world=>ends unless ($you and $me
                and not $them and $their_power{'control world'});

$people=>suffer until (
        $workers->{control}->{means_of_production}++
        and not reverse);

$life=>suffer if not our $communities->{police->{selves}};

$art=>sucks while ($art = $commodity); for (@consumption){not $expression};

alternative_possible:
foreach ($act{'resistance'}) { $our_hope++ and $their_power--; }
die ($corporate_masters . $you. "won't stop us.\n")

__END__

=head1 LICENCE
```

        Copyright (C)2006 **Charlie Harvey**

This program is free software; you can redistribute it and/or
modify it under the terms of the GNU General Public License
as published by the Free Software Foundation; either version
2 of the License, or (at your option) any later version.

This program is distributed in the hope that it will be
useful, but WITHOUT ANY WARRANTY; without even the implied
warranty of MERCHANTABILITY or FITNESS FOR A PARTICULAR
PURPOSE. See the GNU General Public License for more
details.

You should have received a copy of the GNU General Public
License along with this program; if not, write to the Free
Software Foundation, Inc., 59 Temple Place - Suite 330,
Boston, MA 02111-1307, USA.
Also available on line: http://www.gnu.org/copyleft/gpl.html

=cut

from Characters Out In Their Thousands

They walked into the store, some stayed on the ground floor and the rest dispersed throughout the store. Some went up three lots of escalators to the home and soft furnishings department on the top floor. At 2.45pm the cries started breaking out. 'We give thanks to you Selfridges, for the opportunity to consume and consume and buy all I need. And when I'm lost, You give me needs so that I know what I need. You are my guiding light, the way, my path. You are almighty, all-powerful, you give my life meaning.' Some prayers are small and silent in corners of the store. A shopper might stumble across a kneeling body whispering words of adoration.

'Selfridges you fulfill me, come into my life again.' Bodies moving up and down escalators. 60 voices. Security guards rushing from one outbreak to another, ejecting some, but confused when the voices stop in one area and break out in another. 'Hallelujah! Praise be to Selfridges the almighty. You are my lord, I worship you who have saved me from the obscurity of not knowing my purpose in life.' Shoppers stop, product in hand, staring at the bodies. 'Let us hold hands together, brothers and sisters, and raise our voices in thanks to the almighty, amen'

The worshippers leave when the infidels ask them to. Bodies are trembling.

Ceri Buck

The day the world stopped turning

The day the world stopped turning,
a different sort of silence descended from the skies.
No-one bothered to watch the telly although the event was covered live.
In some ways it was an ordinary day just like any other,
 except traffic wardens were joyriding
and no-one gave a toss about the property ladder.

And as we waited for death without a word of protest,
the London and New York stock exchanges became temples of tranquillity.
Suicide rates were remarkably low but very few pubs were empty.
No-one manned the call centres except a couple of under-managers.
People everywhere stopped dieting and Cliff Richard popped his cherry.

No technology was upgraded and no-one went to war.
People shared their innermost secrets but no-one gossiped anymore
and although we collectively lost our pride many found a vestige of self-respect.
No language in the world could do it justice, although Richard and Judy did
 their best,
and Elton John wrote a song to befit the occasion,
but no CD was ever pressed.

The arse dropped out of organised crime and the prisons opened early;
and while yuppies locked themselves indoors and took solace from
 Paul McCartney,
the bookies put odds on anyone surviving at five billion to one,
while therapists in Los Angeles sat their clients down and told them
 they were scum.

The paparazzi deserted celebrities and left them feeling lonely.
Politicians everywhere admitted they were lying
and then went home to spend time with their families.

The UN found itself helpless again but neighbours became friends,
and the advertising industry was racking its brains right until the very end,
but nothing was for sale because nothing was worth buying
and you can't put spin on a world that isn't turning.

Everyone's debts were cancelled and lifestyle became redundant;
sceptics prayed frantically to save their souls,
and the tabloids became indignant,
and launched a last minute campaign to find someone to blame,
whilst trying not to feel upset about a blue green planet swollen with regret,
people flocked to see one last sunset,
but the sunset never came.

In a way it felt like a privilege to be there at the end
and maybe one day we'll do it all over again;
but if anyone ever hears about this they might benefit from learning
that we lived our lives more than ever before
on the day the world stopped turning.

Rob Gee

After the revolution

It was a time I'll always remember
Because I could never forget
How reality fell down around us
Like some Western movie set
And once the dust all settled
The sun shone so bright
And a great calm took over us
Like it was all gonna be alright
That's how it felt to be alive
After the revolution

From Groton to Tacoma
On many a factory floor
The workers talked of solidarity
And refused to build weapons of war
No more will we make missiles
We're gonna do something different
And for the first time
Their children were proud of their parents
And somewhere in Gaza a little boy smiled and cried
After the revolution

Prison doors swung open
And mothers hugged their sons
The Liberty Bell was ringing
When the cops put down their guns
A million innocent people
Lit up in the springtime air
And Mumia and Leonard and Sarah Jane Olson
Took a walk in Tompkins Square
And they talked about what they'd do now
After the revolution

The debts were all forgiven
In all the neo-colonies
And the soldiers left their bases
Went back to their families

And a non-aggression treaty
Was signed with every sovereign state
And all the terrorist groups disbanded
With no empire left to hate
And they all started planting olive trees
After the revolution

George Bush and Henry Kissinger
Were sent off to the World Court
Their plans for global domination
Were pre-emptively cut short
Their weapons of mass destruction
Were inspected and destroyed
The battleships were dismantled
Never again to be deployed
And the world breathed a sigh of relief
After the revolution

Solar panels were on the rooftops
Trains upon the tracks
Organic food was in the markets
No GMOs upon the racks
And all the billionaires
Had to learn how to share
And Bill Gates was told to quit his whining
When he said it wasn't fair
And his mansion became a collective farm
After the revolution

And all the political poets
Couldn't think of what to say
So they all decided
To live life for today
I spent a few years catching up
With all my friends and lovers
Sleeping til eleven
Home beneath the covers
And I learned how to play the accordion
After the revolution

David Rovics

Life's a beach

(Barmouth, summer 2004)

An ebbing curtain reveals the beach.
The stage is set and slowly
the sun lures the actors to their places.

Mam with buggy, toddlers and towels
looks daggers as dad carries his new kite.
Three lads eye the talent
and slyly admire their own
steroid-sculpted bodies.
Ageing skin greets the sun's warmth
like sunflowers - angling deckchairs
for a full blast of rays.
A woman goes topless;
boys stare, so do dads.
Weekday scowls turn to weekend smiles, eyes twinkle.
    No suits.
A game of footie collapses in hysterics
as Fatbelly chases a lost cause of a ball,
trips over an excited dog
and crashes into the sea.
A child squeals excited as the crab
her brother caught glides across her hand
and back into the rock pool.
Ice cream drizzles down chins.
Sandwiches fill with sand.
Bronzed kids leap at the waves,
grandmothers raise their saris in the shallows
as they bring a new generation to baptise.
Everyone pisses in the sea.
    No laptops, no desks, no rules.
But no-one steals as clothes, shoes and towels are left for hours
no-one fights
no-one invades the next family's space.

Everyone respects this common law, our unwritten rules -
rules that don't need parliamentary assent
or a special council by-law.

Children share their shrimp haul, make new friends
in dinghies nobody seems to own,
comparing accents,
invent a new country to impress new friends,
Invent a new past.

A whiff of vinegar and candyfloss reminds the happy horde
of the funfair and beach cafés - across the prom
from their beach. No commerce
breaches the golden sands save
for the donkey rides and trampolines -
donkeys old enough to remember the parents
still gently lope up and down.
The garish waltzer's noise dies
on the sea breeze.
      No suits, no stripes, no status sullies these bronzed bodies.
Now the tide rolls back in.
The boys and girls traipse off to the pub and chippy -
flushed by the sun and the chance of pulling.
Families migrate to the quay to watch
the lobster pots get emptied.
Old couples still slumber in their cars,
in their cardies.
The beach retreats, the tide scours it clean
til tomorrow, when the
happy anarchy will return.

Marc Jones

The Poets

Ebele Ajogbe
...is a Nigerian-born East-Londoner. Loves hugs. Loves mangoes. Her book, 'Poetry is a Woman' is available through her website:
www.ebele.co.uk

David Bateman
...is a self-employed writer-tutor-performer, and a hard-core regular of the Dead Good Poets Society in Liverpool. His poetry publications include 'Curse Of The Killer Hedge' (Iron, 1996) and 'A Homage To Me' (Driftwood, 2003). Another collection, 'More Spit Than Polish', is due from Driftwood.

Marie Berry
...is the editor of KnockBack
www.myspace.com/knockback

Penny Broadhurst
...comes from a small hamlet in the Yorkshire Dales, but currently resides in dirty old Leeds. Yes, Yorkshire, where all those popular beat combos come from. She isn't one of them. If she was, it would be easier. She is a musician, actor, singer, writer and spoken word artist.
www.pennybroadhurst.com

Ceri Buck
...is a poet and site-specific writer, performing and inscribing words and texts in exchange with the urban space.
www.openbracket.org.uk

Alan Buckley
...is a writer and performer living in Oxford. He is one half of the spoken word duo Rhyme and Reason with the very talented Mr George Roberts, and has had poems published in Magma, Orbis, Iota and The Nail. He was winner of the 2005 Oxford Literary Festival Slam, and is currently one of two poets in residence at HMP Grendon

Janis Butler Holm
...teaches experimental writing at Ohio University, where she has served as Associate Editor for Wide Angle, the film journal. 'Memo to Barbie' first appeared in the Canadian magazine _Tessera_.

Ken Champion
...is a widely published poet who has appeared in over eighty magazines and anthologies both in the UK and the USA. His collection 'Cameo Poly' is published by Tall Lighthouse.

Danny Chivers
...is trying to, like, save the world and stuff using the combined powers of ludicrous misadventure, irritating cheerfulness, and, most recently, pie charts. To maintain his naive day-to-day enthusiasm in the face of mass global inequality and looming climate mayhem, he writes poetry in which he sometimes gets a bit cross.

Spencer Cooke
...is a getting on a bit. He's been writing poetry for years, but can't be bothered trying to get it published, and thinks most of it is rubbish anyway. Whilst he thinks art is important and everything, he doesn't think it's as important as three feet of sea level rise or, more importantly, that it will really do much to prevent it. He is a fully paid up grumpy cynic who lives by himself on the fringes of civilised society with a growing collection of Wagner on vinyl and a set of very sharp knives. He's a Yorkshireman, but will attempt to be sociable if you buy him a pint, and may even cook you dinner if you're lucky.

M T C Cronin
...has published twelve collections of poetry (the most recent being 'The Flower, The Thing', UQP, 2006), including several in translation and her work has won and been shortlisted for many major literary awards. She currently lives in Maleny, Australia, with her partner and three young daughters.

B R Dionysius
...is a poet, editor, and educator. He has three collections of poetry, 'Fatherlands' (Five Islands Press, 2000), 'Bacchanalia' (Interactive Press, 2002) and the verse novel 'Universal Andalusia' (SOI3 Press, 2006, www.papertigermedia.com). He was short-listed in the 2002 Mary Gilmore Poetry Prize for Fatherlands. He lives in Brisbane, Australia. 'The Conference of the (under)employed Birds' was previously published in Blackmail Press NZ, and 'These Gifts (ii)' won second place in the Greater Dandenong Open Poetry Prize, 2004.

Josh Ekroy
...is a London based poet and has had work published in numerous anthologies, magazines and competitions including third place in the Red Pepper / Iraq Occupation Focus poetry competition on the theme of war and occupation.

Kate Evans

...has been marrying words and images for political effect for the last ten years. She is an active environmental campaigner and has written and published 'Copse, a cartoon history of the roads protest movement in the UK' and 'Funny Weather' a graphic guide to global warming.
www.cartoonkate.co.uk

Claire Fauset

...aka Radical Supergirly is a performance poet, activist and researcher for Corporate Watch. Her poetry is online at **www.re-clairethestreets.blogspot.com** and her political writing is at **www.corporatewatch.org.uk**

Rob Gee

Performance poet, comic, and reformed psychiatric nurse, Rob has been commissioned to write poetry for Leicester City Football Club and BBC Radio, won several poetry slams and been published in numerous anthologies. His is the only performance to have instigated a fight at Leamington Spa Peace Festival and he is sometimes sent into schools as a warning to children.
www.robgee.co.uk

Heidi Greco

...is an editor and writer whose poems have appeared in a range of magazines and anthologies. She also writes book reviews for newspapers and magazines. Heidi lives in South Surrey, BC, Canada in a house surrounded by trees. Her published work includes the books 'Siren Tattoo' and 'Rattlesnake Plantain' (Anvil Press).
www.outonthebiglimb.blogspot.com

Michelle Green

'Her social soul poetry reaches into your heart and your head and makes them do the twist together.' Michelle is a performer, poet, storyteller, regional slam champion and occasional zine maker and distributor based in Manchester. Her book 'Knee High Affairs' is published by Crocus Books.
www.myspace.com/kneehighaffairs

Mark Gunnery

...is a songwriter, activist and organiser from South Berkley, California. He is currently working on a zine distro called Wasted Earth and is a member of Riot Folk, a collective of radical artists and musicians.
www.riotfolk.org

Mark Gwynne Jones

John Cooper Clarke said of Mark: *'I always stipulate that who ever is on with me hasn't got to be any good - this one got past me - I don't know how, but heads will roll.'* Mark performs with his band Mark Gwynne Jones and the Psychicbread. 'Plastic Man' appears in his collection 'Psychicbread' (Route Publications) and on his CD 'in the light of this'.
www.psychicbread.org

Rosemary Harris

...is a writer and performer, who has appeared at Glastonbury Festival, BAC, Soho Writers' Festival and on Radio 3. She has been published in numerous poetry magazines and won 1st prize in 2004's Middlesex University International Poetry Competition; and was commended in the 2005 National Poetry Competition. Rosemary was writer for the award-winning 'Sardines - The Musical', which premiered at London's Sadlers' Wells Theatre in September 2006.

Charlie Harvey

...is a free software advocate, activist and computer geek. He enjoys punk rock, dub reggae and good cider. If we had to live in places that were anagrams of our names, he would live in Hierarchy Vale. But in fact he lives in Oxford. He has no plans to change his name to Rod Fox. Though he concedes that it does sound rather dashing.

Mathew Herbert

You could say that 'Matthew is to poetry what Unilever is to greenwash', but it'd be a lie. Matthew' day job is about enabling grassroots activists to work together more co-operatively and take more dynamic direct action <**www.seedsforchange.org.uk**>. Enough of the shameless plugs. Step away from the ice cream (the cows will thank you for it) and go take back the streets.

Kevin Higgins

...is the author of poetry collection 'The Boy With No Face' (2005). Kevin teaches poetry workshops at Galway Arts Centre and is co-organiser of the 'Over The Edge: Open Reading series' in Galway, Ireland. 'Portrait of The Boss...' was originally published in Metre magazine.

John Hoggett
...has lived in Reading for over twenty years, has historical links to the artistic elite of this country and is immensely talented.

Will Holloway
...studied at the Conservatoire Ancien de la Poésie under Léopold Argot where he took the Prix des Prix in circumlocution. His poetry is measured at 78.2 Gigasublimities. His collections 'President McVeigh' (2004) and 'Suicide Bombing is just so Passive-Aggressive' (2005) were both short-listed for the Helios. He has been commissioned by BBC Radio Four to denounce the system and he has performed at The Coltan, The Witz and many other venues too cool for you to have heard of. His dad is an astronaut.
www.willholloway.com

Philip Jeays
...is a singer and songwriter with a biting wit, a tender heart and a raging lust for life. He writes lyrics that are clear, literate and evocative, drawing on the legacy of sharp sarcy social comment pioneered by Jacques Brel. If Withnail was a singer he'd be Philip Jeays.
www.jeays.com

Marc Jones
...is a Welsh socialist republican, having been active in the miners' strike and anti-poll tax campaigns. Most recently he's been campaigning against Liverpool councils dumping their waste in Wales. He co-edits Red Poets, an annual collection of Welsh radical poets.

Steve Larkin
...is the 2004 International Spoken Word Olympic Champion. Funny and gritty, thoughtful and foul, Steve is a founder and compere of the UK's largest poetry slam, Hammer & Tongue. Steve Larkin has recorded one album 'The Midas Touch and Other Curses'.
www.stevelarkin.co.uk

Emma Lee
...has a poetry collection called 'Yellow Torchlight and the Blues' available from Original Plus. Her poems have been nominated for Forward Prizes, widely published and performed in venues such as Leicester City Football Club. She lives in Leicester with her husband Paul and small daughter.

Jeffrey Mackie
...is a poet from Montreal, Canada. His work has been widely published both in Canada and internationally. Mackie's latest collection 'Graffiti Scripture' 2002 is now available from Onanist Press.

Paul Maltby

...is a professor of postmodern fiction, postmodern critique, and postmodern film at West Chester University. His piece is an extract from his novel 'The Occupation'. Paul is also author of two critical studies: 'Dissident Postmodernists' (University of Pennsylvania Press, 1991) and 'The Visionary Moment: A Postmodern Critique' (State University of New York Press, 2002).

Aoife Mannix

...is an Irish writer and poet. Her first collection of poetry 'The Elephant In The Corner' was published by Tall Lighthouse (www.tall-lighthouse.co.uk) in July 2005. You can also read some of her writing at **www.editred.com/ aoifemannix** or visit her own website **www.aoifemannix.com**.

Alan McClure

...is a ranger at an organic farm/visitor centre in Dumfries and Galloway, where he lives with his partner and one year old son. He has been writing and performing songs for ten years or so, some of which can be found at **www.myspace.com/alanmcclure**.

Elvis McGonagall

... ('one man and his doggerel') a stand-up poet, armchair revolutionary and recumbent rocker, Elvis McGonagall is the sole resident of The Graceland Caravan Park somewhere near Dundee where he scribbles verse whilst drinking malt whisky, listening to Johnny Cash and throwing heavy objects at his portable telly. Elvis is the 2006 World Slam Champion and currently appears as a regular guest poet on BBC Radio 4's "Saturday Live". He is compere of the notorious Blue Suede Sporran Club.
www.elvismcgonagall.co.uk

Ben Mellor

...is a writer, performer and educator, originally from down south, currently residing up north. He has performed poetry all over the country and is now developing his first solo show, Voices of Dissent, for touring in Autumn 2007. This will be the debut production of his arts company Moksha. The poem in this collection is the first he has had published and one of his short stories was recently published by Route in their 'Brief Lives' collection.

Merrick

...when he can get his tattooed arse out of bed, is a political writer, ecological activist and master of mayhem. He is author of the book 'Battle for the Trees' about the Newbury Bypass campaign, and his team projects include the publishing coolective Godhaven Ink and anarchic audio monganauts Radio Savage Houndy Beasty
www.rshb.org.uk
bristlingbadger.blogspot.com

Adrian Mitchell

...is 'a poet who would stalk the powerful, the pretentious and the sycophantic' and the UK's Shadow Poet Laureate. 'Advertising Will Eat the World' and 'Pioneers, O Pioneers' are published in Adrian's 2004 collection, 'The Shadow Knows: Poems 2001 - 2004', Bloodaxe Books.
www.rippingyarns.co.uk/adrian

Helen Moore

...is an eco-poet/environmental writer based near Bath, in Somerset, South-west England.
www.natureswords.co.uk

Dave Morgan

...was turned on to poetry after winning a plastic army lorry for reciting 'I had a little pony' at the Coronation celebrations in his local pub, aged 5. He is co-founder of 'Write Out Loud' promoting poetry performance in the North West of England.
www.writeoutloud.net

Gregg Mosson

...from the US was recently published in Attic, Poets' Ink, and Perpetuum Mobile, and he publishes the annual magazine Poems Against War: A Journal of Poetry and Action.

Cath Morris

... is an Ottawa-born English tutor and poet, Cath continues to write poetry, she is awaiting publication of her first chapbook from above/ground press in Ottawa.

Alistair Noon

His poems have been published in magazines and anthologies from Chicago to Tokyo, and online at nthposition.com and Litter. He coordinates the annual Poetry Hearings festival in Berlin. 'I have decided' was previously published in 'The Ugly Tree'.

This poem is SPONSORED by...

Ewuare X. Osayande
...is a US activist, poet and author. Ewuare Osayande's latest book 'Blood Luxury' is published internationally by Africa World Press. His is co-founder of POWER, People Organised Working to Eradicate Racism.
ww.osayande.org

Rachel Pantechnicon
...writes mainly for her cat Harold, but some of her work also appeals to humans. Her favourite book is 'Collins Rhyming Dictionary'.
www.rachelpantechnicon.com

Mario Petrucci
...is considered one of Britain's most versatile and innovative poets. Petrucci's Arvon prize-winning collection 'Heavy Water: a poem for Chernobyl' (Enitharmon) is now available as a film (www.seventh-art.com) marking the 20th anniversary of the Chernobyl disaster.
http://mariopetrucci.port5.com.

Emma Philips
...is a primary school teacher from Devon. She has had work highly commended in the Oxfam Poetry Competition 2004, Red Pepper/Iraq Occupation Focus Competition 2005 and her work appears in the 2006 Bluechrome Poetry Competition Anthology.

George Roberts
...from Oxford is one half of poetry duo Rhyme and Reason, with the better half, Alan Buckley. He performs regularly at the Hammer & Tongue poetry slams and at venues even Elvis hasn't been seen at. His poems have appeared in Fire, Magma and The Nail.
http://georgeroberts.livejournal.com.

David Rovics
...has been called the musical voice of the progressive movement in the US. He will make you laugh, he will make you cry, and he will make the revolution irresistible. All of his recordings are available for free download on his website,
www.davidrovics.com.

Sheena Salmon
...began her spoken word career in the plush surroundings of London's premier squats, she continues to perform in liberated venues and festivals across the country. A freelance writer and stand-up comedian Sheena is a regular performer on the London comedy circuit, and runs workshops for young people outside of mainstream eduacation. Contact Sheena at sheenasalmon1@hotmail.com

K Simpson
... anarchist, doctor, poet and punk musician of Wellington, New Zealand. Singer/ guitarist in Dead Vicious, an old-school punk band famous in Newtown and Berhampore. He is married to Anne MacLennan. He has no children, apart from himself.

Paul Spencer
...combines two family traditions of music and radical politics. He has been semi-transient since 1998 and currently lives at sea-level fretting about climate change. He has ties to Australia and Yorkshire. He recently spent six months getting from England to Australia.
www.paulspencer.org.

Spoz
...is an award winning performance poet, singer / songwriter, filmmaker and playwright. He is a member of the New October Poets and is the poet in residence at Birmingham City FC and currently Birmingham's Poet Laureate.
www.spoz.net

Alistair Stewart
...is the author of 'Frankston 281' and writes poems for the Mangowak Football Academy. He lives in Melbourne, Australia with his son Sam.

Stig
...is not yet a poet, but helped us by designing this book for free. He's worked with Corporate Watch and a host of other grass-roots groups and NGOs for over 10 years as a graphic designer, prop-maker and illustrator.
www.shtig.net

Attila the Stockbroker
...the sharp tongued, high energy, social surrealist rebel poet and songwriter. Attila has published 4 books of poems: 'Cautionary Tales for Dead Commuters' (Unwin, 1985) 'Scornflakes' (Bloodaxe, 1992) 'The Rat Tailed Maggot' (Roundhead, 1998) and 'Goldstone Ghosts' (2001)
www.attilathestockbroker.com

Todd Swift
...is the author of three poetry collections and editor of many poetry anthologies, including '100 Poets Against The War', 'Future Welcome' and 'Babylon Burning'. He compiled the recent audio CD 'Life Lines: Poets for Oxfam'. He has been poetry editor of online magazine Nthposition since 2002 and Oxfam GB Poet In Residence since 2004. He is editing an anthology of twentieth-century Canadian poetry for Carcanet. His latest publication is 'Natural Curve', a pamphlet of poems (Rubicon Press).
http://toddswift.blogspot.com

This poem is SPONSORED by...

Steve Tasane

From Cheltenham Festival of Literature to Ken Livingstone's RISE Festival, Steve Tasane's poetry bridges radicalism and populism with rap-funk polemics. Pioneer of contemporary live poetry and innovator of Channel 4's Litpop Festival, Steve also hosted Soho Theatre's Pure Poetry season and has recently toured the UK with his acclaimed one man show Klepto.

Heather Taylor

...is a Canadian writer, performer & educator, who has been published and featured throughout Europe and North America. As a playwright, her work has been seen at the Tricycle, Soho Theatre, Greenwich, the Pleasance, & Theatre 503. Her full collection 'Horizon & Back' is published by Tall Lighthouse (www.tall-lighthouse.co.uk). www.heathertaylor.co.uk

The Speech Painter

...has performed poetry for 15 years, from co-founding of poetry's first pop group Atomic Lip to co-running Pure Poetry at Soho Theatre, London. He is winner of many poetry slams and can be found online at **www.speechpainter.com**

Helên Thomas

...performs regularly throughout the UK. She organises poetry events for the Lymm Festival and for Hot Wire Poetry events. As part of performance poetry duo 'We Are Poets!' she takes performance poetry into schools and provides workshops for children in writing, roleplay and performance.
www.creativewomensnetwork.co.uk/CWNWeArePoets

Jim Thomas

...has performed all over the world from Australia and the Philippines to the USA and even Outer Mongolia. He is 2006 Capital Slam Champion (Ottawa, Canada) and co-founder of the Hammer & Tongue slam in Oxford, UK. By day Jim is a technology activist, writer and researcher for the ETC Group and he is based in Montreal, Canada.
http://jimsnail.blogspot.com

Vincent Tinguely

...is a Montreal writer and performance poet. He is the co-author of 'Impure', a book about the Montreal spoken word scene. He writes regularly on spoken word and lit events for the free weekly Montreal Mirror. He has published a three chapbook set 'SEX, POWER, MYTH' and a mini-CD 'Flying Under The Radar'. He co-published the zine Perfect Waste of Time vol. 2, no. 2, and his novella, 'Final Trainwreck of a Lost-Mind Summer', was self-published in August 2005.
http://randomgeneration.blogspot.com

T Troughton

... has written poetry, books, features and investigative journalism. She currently lives in Ireland and Walthamstow.

Nick Toczek

...has been a professional writer and performer for the past forty years. He is a poet, storyteller, magician, puppeteer, journalist and stand-up comedian. Nick has published numerous books & recordings, most recently 'Group of Heroes' (Skrev Press) & the CD 'Selfish Men'.

Janet Vickers

...has been published in journals such as sub-Terrain and Grain, and in anthologies such as Down in the Valley and Common Sky: Canadian writers against the war. She lives in Abbotsford, BC Canada.

Rapunzel Wizard

...is an environmental activist as well as a performance poet, mixing comedy and politics in his verse. He has performed everywhere from a muddy field at Glastonbury Festival, to a muddy field at Newbury Bypass protest. He has moved to Aberdeenshire to find new muddy fields to gig in.

Luke Wright

...is a member of the 'Poetry Boyband' group Aisle 16. His poems are a cut-and-paste extravaganza of the stuff we read and know, colouring in the monoculture with sarcastic disco lights. Wright is curator of poetry at Whitechapel Art Gallery. 'If (Rebranded)' is published in 'Live From The Hellfire Club' by Aisle16 (Egg Box Books, 2005).
www.lukewright.co.uk

Christian Zorka

...is the author of 'Sièges' (a book of poems in French), edited by Le Quartanier (Montreal, Canada) and of texts in various journals. The poems published here are part of an ongoing series titled 'Turning out your pockets'. Zorka currently lives in New York.
www.christianzorka.com

What is Corporate Watch?

Corporations have gained a power out of all proportion to their original purpose. Corporate Watch is a radical, independent, research group supporting the campaigns which are increasingly successful in forcing corporations to back down and dragging the corrupt links between business and power, economics and politics into the spotlight. Corporate Watch is part of the growing anti-corporate movement springing up around the world.

From Corporate Watch's beginnings looking at PFI roadbuilding, we have broadened out to examine the oil industry, globalisation, genetic engineering, food, toxic chemicals, privatisation and many other areas, to build up a picture of almost every type of corporate crime and the nature and mechanisms of corporate power, both economic and political. We have worked with and provided information to empower peace campaigners, environmentalists, and trade unionists; large NGOs and small autonomous groups; journalists, MPs, and members of the public.

Over ten years we have transformed a loose association of activists and researchers into a respected professional research and campaigning organisation, run effectively as a workers' co-operative.

What Corporate Watch does:

Website
Our website provides the latest news, detailed profiles of some of the world's largest corporations and overviews of each major industry sector. It constitutes not just a resource for campaigners and journalists but also aims to provide a comprehensive picture of the reality of our corporate age.

www.corporatewatch.org.uk

Newsletter
Our bi-monthly newsletter provides the best in corporate critical journalism, with stories covering virtually every corporate sector and every type corporate crime.

Information and outreach

We regularly give talks and workshops on all areas of our work. We also advise campaigners on corporate issues and try to make our work as accessible and useful as possible.

Food and Farming project

This project aims to raise awareness of the unchecked consolidation of corporate control of food production and its negative impact on society and the environment. It aims to support activists, farmers and the general public in resisting corporate control of the food industry and and creating sustainable local food systems.

Corporate Structures project

This project looks into the legal basis of corporate structures, rights and duties, in order to analyse how legal rights and obligations influence corporate behaviour and what changes must be made to corporate structures (or what structures must replace corporations) in order for corporate social responsibility to become a reality instead of a PR buzzword.

Public Relations Industry project

PR campaigns reinforce corporate power and work against democracy. Through deception and deceit the public relations industry reduces society's capacity to respond effectively to key social, environmental and political challenges. This project aims to deepen understanding of this little known industry, how it operates, and how to combat it.

If you would like to support us, or find out more, please get in touch:

> Corporate Watch
> 16b Cherwell Street
> Oxford
> OX4 1BG
> United Kingdom

mail@corporatewatch.org
www.corporatewatch.org.uk

Other publications by Corporate Watch

Here are brief descriptions of some of the most popular reports, briefings and booklets produced by Corporate Watch. The best way we can counter corporate rule is to get informed, to share ideas, tactics and plans, and then to work together. You can order these publications or subscribe to the bi-monthly Corporate Watch Newsletter by writing to us, or through our online shop.
www.corporatewatch.org.uk

Prices listed below include postage & packaging to a UK address. For orders to a European address please add 10% to your order total. For orders to an address outside Europe please add 25%. Send a cheque payable to 'Corporate Watch' with your name and address, to:

Corporate Watch
16b Cherwell Street,
Oxford OX4 1BG UK

Being designed at time of going to press

Nanotech: Undersized, Under regulated and already here!

An overview of how corporations in the UK are commercialising nanotech products. It asks what are nanomaterials? Why are they made? Who makes them? What products are they used in? What are the dangers? And where are the regulations?
January 2007 - A4 - £3.00

What's Wrong With Corporate Social Responsibility?

With all the hype about 'Corporate Social Responsibility', the question is, are companies really changing their tune? Or is it all greenwash and PR? Corporate Watch's report 'What's Wrong with Corporate Social Responsibility' tells you what companies really get out of CSR and why their empty rhetoric is not to be trusted.
May 2006 - 32 pages A4 - £3.00

Checkout Chuckout
DIY guide to stopping supermarket developments
This guide gives an overview of what happens when a supermarket threatens to move into your town, and also details the planning and campaigning tools, tactics and inspiration that you can use to oppose them.
May 2006 - 68 pages A5 - £3.00

Corporate Carve-up
The role of UK corporations in Iraq,
March 2003 - March 2006
The first comprehensive listing of British companies involvement in Iraq. The report reveals that British companies are playing a major part in the effort to create an Iraqi economy based on neoliberal, pro-corporate principles.
March 2006 - 32 pages A4 - £5.00

Corporate Identity
A critical analysis of private companies engagement with the identity cards scheme
Which companies are preparing to bid for contracts under the ID cards scheme? What could be the consequences of technology failures for the ID cards scheme? Find out in our report on corporate involvement with the ID cards scheme.
January 2006 - 16 pages A4 - £3.00

149   This poem is SP0N$0R3D by...

Nanotechnology
What is it and how corporations are using it
Nanotechnology, the manipulation of matter at the scale of atoms and molecules, has been described both as the next industrial revolution and as the operating system for a new era of corporate and state control.
March 2005 - 4 pages A4 - £1.00

What's Wrong with Supermarkets
Strip lights, endless queues of strangers and shelves of packets, fake smiles from bored checkout assistants - isn't there a better way to get our food? This briefing gives the lowdown on the damage supermarkets are inflicting on communities and ecosystems in the UK and across the world, and what we can do about it.
5th edition: June 2004 - 40 pages A5 - £3.00
We have also produced a summary of this booklet that is four A4 pages and costs just £1.00

A Rough Guide to the UK Farming Crisis
Farming is in crisis. Farmers complain that despite subsidies they cannot make ends meet, that they are paid less than production costs and many are being driven into bankruptcy.
May 2004 - 52 pages A4 - £6.00

Other publications by Corporate Watch

Corporate law and structures
Exposing the roots of the problem

The way corporations work is not a law of nature but something that we have the power to change. This briefing, exposes what makes corporations tick, legally, and explains how corporations have developed, why corporations should not be seen as 'persons' in law and how the legal duties of corporate directors mean that companies can only be interested in profit.
January 2004 - 32 pages A4 - £3.00

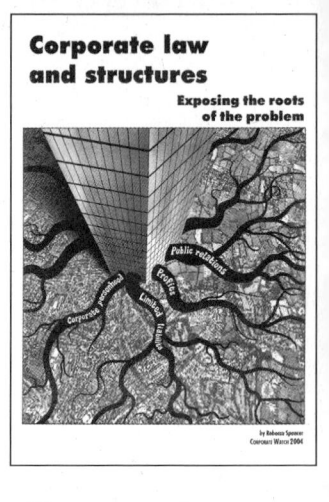

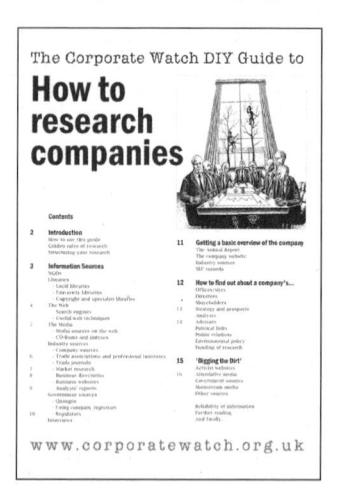

How to Research Corporations

Successful campaigns to tackle corporate abuse need to have the facts behind them. The Corporate Watch DIY Guide covers everything all campaigners need to know about researching companies, from internet based research, to using libraries and conducting interviews.
June 2002 - 16 pages A4 - £1.50

Become a friend of Corporate Watch

Corporate Watch runs on a shoestring budget and we rely on donations from supporters to keep going. A £10 a month standing order will make you a 'Friend of Corporate Watch'. You will receive all of our publications and newsletters. Sign up online at www.corporatewatch.org.uk